Bibliographic Instruction:

A Handbook

By Beverly Renford and
Linnea Hendrickson

WITHDRAWN
FROM STOCK

Neal-Schuman Publishers, Inc.

14447

Published by Neal-Schuman Publishers Inc.
64 University Place
New York, New York 10003

Copyright © 1980 by Neal-Schuman Publishers, Inc.

All rights reserved. Reproduction of this book, in whole or in part, without written permission of the publisher is prohibited.

Printed and bound in the United States of America.

Distributed outside North America by
Mansell Publishing
3 Bloomsbury Place
London WC1A 2QA, England

Library of Congress Cataloging in Publication Data

Renford, Beverly.
Bibliographic instruction.

Bibliography: p.
1. Library orientation—Handbooks, manuals, etc.
I. Hendrickson, Linnea, joint author. II. Title.
Z711.2.R38 025.5′6 80-12300
ISBN 0-918212-24-3

Coláiste
Mhuire Gan Smal
Luimneach
Class No. 025.56
Acc. No. 94586

DEDICATION

To all instructional librarians—
past, present and forever

Contents

Preface

Not too many years ago, a library administrator was heard to say that bibliographic instruction was simply a fad, and like all such ephemeral things, would eventually fade away. This prediction has shown little sign of being proved true. In fact, academic library instruction has experienced phenomenal growth and has become an expected function within the library.

Like data-base searching and networking, library instruction was a foreign activity for many of the working librarians. Few felt adequately prepared to take on bibliographic instruction without some guidance. To compensate for their lack of formal training, librarians concerned with instruction flocked to workshops and conferences. These same individuals were instrumental in organizing national, state, and regional structures that centered on the issues of bibliographic instruction.

At the same time that formalized activities were being organized, colleagues who were already involved in exciting and often innovating programs began to communicate through the library literature. The books, articles, and reports that resulted were quite helpful in generating enthusiasm and new ideas. It is in this same spirit of collegial communication that *Bibliographic Instruction: A Handbook* was written.

This book is intended to serve as a practical guide for

those involved in developing or improving library-user education programs and activities. The information included in each chapter has been based upon first-hand experience and research. The book may be read in its entirety for an overview or be consulted a section at a time on whatever aspect of bibliographic instruction is of interest.

All of the major types of library instruction activities have been included: planning, orientation, printed guides, course-related/integrated courses, credit courses, workbooks, and computer-assisted instruction. These topics have been arranged from the most basic to the most complex instructional activities. This does not mean, however, that it is necessary for a program to move from orientation to computer-assisted instruction. In fact, many libraries have successfully combined a variety of activities to form a wholesome program.

The key issues in the development and implementation of the various activities have been discussed, and appropriate examples and samples have been included. The suggested readings listed at the end of each chapter have been carefully selected for their usefulness and applicability. For those desiring further information, additional sources have been included in the Appendix.

One final note is in order. This book does not attempt to establish definitive answers to the many questions involved in bibliographic instruction. Rather, it suggests possible solutions and modes of operation, and serves as a guide for thinking about specific programs in specific libraries.

Viva bibliographic instruction!

CHAPTER 1

Planning for an Instructional Program

Bibliographic instruction is often considered a "grass roots" service started by reference or undergraduate librarians who perceived an instructional program as the solution to many of the problems they encountered daily at the service desks. When waves of students presented themselves at the reference desk, the staff found itself repeating the same information over and over again to students attempting to complete assignments requiring library work. Often these students possessed insufficient knowledge of the library to successfully pursue the projects, and it became apparent that "something had to be done" to meet their needs in an organized, efficient fashion.

In addition to the obvious needs of the students within the library, faculty became instrumental in the establishment of formal library instruction. Certain instructors regularly requested library tours for their classes, apparently believing that a tour would thoroughly prepare the students to use the library. Librarians, realizing the limitations of the tour, began to combine instructional sessions on basic library skills and materials with the tour.

Aside from the infrequent requests of the teaching faculty, library instruction programs generally evolved as a result of the needs perceived by the library staff. The classes or patrons that were obviously having problems within the library became the target for formal instruction. Library users received library instruction largely by chance, depending on whether they were enrolled in a particular class. This shotgun approach often resulted in unbalanced programs, and instructional librarians have started to recognize the weakness of operating in this fashion. It has become obvious that library instruction programs must be planned and not left to chance.

When the planning process is started for either beginning or existing instructional programs, it is essential that there be an accurate assessment of the existing situation. The word accurate is stressed here because librarians have tended to react to symptoms rather than causes. Lubans pointed out the weakness of such thinking when he wrote:

> Most library-use instruction is based on what we as librarians *think* library users need to know. It is this educated guesswork or *perceived need* on which many programs (tours, orientation lectures, a multitude of multimedia presentations or formal courses in bibliography) have been based. Since we are prompted to action by what we observe is lacking in the library users at the time of the user's need, our response is apt to be a type of bibliographic first aid.[1]

In attempting to put together what is virtually a case study of the library, its academic community, and their relationship to each other, there are many areas that should be examined. This can be best accomplished by asking and answering a number of meaningful questions about both. For example, what is the overall attitude of the library staff toward instruction? Is library administration willing to support efforts by providing release time, money, and personnel? Are there individuals willing and able to teach? Is there sufficient personnel for specific activities such as guided tours or course-related classes and seminars? Does the library have the physical facilities for classroom instruction? What equipment is available to support instructional efforts?

In looking outside the library, close attention should be paid to those things that affect the services offered to the academic community. How many students are enrolled? What percentage are registered for full-time study? Part-time study? How many students commute? Live on campus? Are in special programs? Are members of a minority group? What is the number of undergraduates? Graduates? Alternative students? What is the enrollment of the various curriculums? What classes demand research papers? Are there required courses that must be completed by all matriculating students? What faculty members are supportive of the library?

Although it is quite beneficial to find out what other academic institutions are doing, each library must determine the needs of its academic community and then plan accordingly. One library may successfully combine self-guided tours, course-related instruction, and printed handouts. Another library may bypass all three activities and concentrate on a credit program. What may be an exciting, well-organized program for a small liberal arts college, may be a disaster for a large state university.

To illustrate how different situations can affect programs, let's take a detailed look at two very different academic institutions. Institution A is a four-year liberal arts college. It is well known for its premed and prelaw curriculum. Its language program is strong with a third-year abroad option. Enrollment is between 1,500–2,000 students. Institution B is a state university located in a large city. The academic programs are many and varied. A large number of students are enrolled through continuing education. The full-time day students are predominantly commuters. Enrollment varies between 12,000–14,000 FTE's, and there is an open-admission policy.

To say that both these institutions should plan similar library programs would be a mistake. Institution A would be quite successful with a required credit course on library skills. Also, course-related sessions with the biology, political science, or history classes would be easy to initiate. If the library is not large, it may not be necessary to offer guided or self-guided tours.

On the other hand, Institution B will find it necessary to have a variety of library instruction activities. Printed handouts and a self-guided tour will help to meet the needs of the part-time and continuing education students. Both evening and daytime seminars can be used to reach those students taking classes that require papers. A library skills workbook program can work well with the freshmen or with those students enrolled in a basic skills or remediation program.

FINDING ANSWERS TO QUESTIONS

Surprisingly, a wealth of information can be found about the library and the academic community by looking in the right places. There are two or three key offices on most campuses that keep detailed records and statistics. The admissions office will be able to supply student enrollment figures. This would include new, returning, and transfer students. Additional analysis is often provided on residential, commuting, minority, and special-admission students. Statistical summaries for the last two or three years can provide an overall picture of the present student body.

The office for academic affairs is a good source for information on curriculum and programs. It normally disseminates its information through the college catalog or bulletin. These publications provide current information on degree requirements, and should be required reading for the library instructional planner. This same office can often provide additional statistics on the enrollments in specific colleges and departments, and detailed information on special programs such as basic skills or developmental year.

The purpose of obtaining such information is to find out who the library is serving. If, for example, there is a formally recognized remediation program, the library could make every effort to become involved with the students at this level by becoming involved with the program. If there is a high percentage of dormitory residents, evening and weekend workshops or seminars will have a potential audience. If the campus population commutes, the time slots chosen for instructional activities are critical. Will a commuting day student return for an evening activity? With a large continuing education program it is advisable to provide self-guided materials or printed handouts since many of these students use the library during the off hours.

In looking at the degree requirements, be alert for those courses that everyone must take. These can be targeted for organized instructional activity. Also, key courses in the sciences, engineering, business, education, or liberal arts can be effectively used for course-related instruction. Courses that are specifically described as research methods courses are ideal candidates for library instruction. If a credit structure is being considered, find out where such courses will fit into the overall degree picture. Will they be required or elected? Is there room for an additional requirement or will there have to be significant shifts in all majors?

With minimal effort, available information can be gathered from the appropriate offices. Most campuses should have offices comparable to admissions, academic affairs, continuing education, residential life, and graduate student affairs. By using the information and statistics kept in these areas, a bibliographic instruction planner can find answers to many of the questions previously listed.

In addition to this information gathered from sources outside the library, there is much available from within. Libraries are notorious for their assiduous compilation of statistics and record keeping in such areas as circulation, reserves, and reference. Figures from these sources provide raw data on the use patterns of the library. How much does the faculty use the library? What group of students borrow most heavily? What classifications receive the highest circulation? Are reference questions mostly directional in nature? What type of reference questions are being asked? Is there a pattern to the questions? What hours are the busiest at the public service desks? Slowest?

In looking for courses that would benefit from library instruction, the circulation figures are helpful. Heavy circulation of a particular classification (excluding the Dewey 800s and the Library of Congress P's) can be an indication of paper requirements. Reference statistics can provide detailed information about recurrent questions. If there are patterns to the questions being asked, class instructors should be contacted about the possibilities of a library session. Room count statistics will show what blocks of time tend to be the busiest. Term-paper clinics, seminars, or tours will be most successful if they are offered during the hours the students normally use the library.

The whole idea, whether looking inside or outside the library, is to use the records and information available to form a foundation and rationale for developing, changing, or upgrading library instruction. Decisions that are made can be based on the real needs that exist rather than the needs that have been perceived by the library staff.

USER SURVEYS

In addition to the information gathered from the various sources just mentioned, it is possible to conduct a formal survey. The idea is to find out who is using the library and what services these individuals feel they need. A very good example of a user survey completed for the purposes of organizing for instruction was completed by the General Libraries at the University of Texas at Austin. The questionnaires used and the results were included in a publication entitled *A Comprehensive Program of User Education for The General Libraries.*[2] This study should not be missed by those considering a user survey for their library instruction program.

Obviously, formal surveys such as this one cannot be accomplished overnight. They take careful thought and planning. Consideration must also be given to the time and money available for such a project. Although this is an excellent method for gathering accurate and current information, some libraries are not in a position to carry out such an ambitious project.

ADMINISTRATIVE SUPPORT

In some libraries, bibliographic instruction has begun "in spite of the administration." Such a negative environment does little to encourage improvement and growth. The administration has the power to make or break any library activity, and this includes instruction. Maintaining good working relations with the administration is essential, and this can be accomplished by following three key rules.

The first one is to communicate. All administrators have a need to know what is going on in the library. Library instruction activities are not excluded from the list. In many cases, the budget and personnel matters are the responsibility of the top managers. These individuals must be aware of the various program needs for planning purposes. Does the instructional program have equipment needs? Will new staffing be needed to support a workbook program? Will handbooks, bookmarks, or guided tours be printed in bulk? How much will this cost? What does the proposed new instructional activity mean in terms of time, personnel, and money?

The second rule is to work within the proper administrative channels. There is often a middle manager between the instructional librarian and the top library administrator. These individuals hold such positions as department head, head of the undergraduate library, or head of public service. It is with these individuals that communication should begin, for they are most aware of the limitations and assets of their units or departments. Can the reference staff absorb forty sections of the English writing classes every term? If release time is required, who will fill in for the individual being released? Does the reference budget include enough to buy audiovisual (AV) equipment for course-related instruction? The department head is in the best position to answer such questions. It is the middle managers who must carry the library instructional message to the upper administration, so it behooves the instructional librarian to gain them as staunch allies by working with them.

The third rule for gaining administrative support is to keep the various activities visible. Send complimentary copies of bookmarks, self-guided tours, or handbooks to administration members. Pass on complimentary letters from faculty and students to the director. Do not hesitate to ask individual administrators to participate in seminar series, open houses, or orientation tours. Offer to work with special interest groups. Invite the administration to attend appropriate conferences and workshops that relate to instruction. Offer to write up reports of the year's activities for the annual report. It should be remembered that anything (including instruction) that makes the library look good, reflects on its administration.

There will, of course, be administrators who will refuse to recognize or support library instruction. There is no easy solution to such a situation. Individuals finding themselves with such a problem often continue with a minimal amount of instructional activity that is tolerated by administration. Over a period of time, a case for library instruction can be built through supporting letters from faculty and students, and the determined efforts of those dedicated to the concept of bibliographic instruction.

CAMPUS FACULTY AND LIBRARY INSTRUCTION

One of the key ingredients for a successful library instruction program is faculty support. Unless the faculty recognizes the importance of the library and incorporates this belief into course requirements, there is little demand for bibliographic instruction. For those instructional programs just beginning, it is highly desirable that a core of library-oriented faculty be identified. It is with the help of these individuals that programs can flourish, since many of them will be quite receptive to any activity that furthers their own interests. How can such individuals be found? There is always personal contact. Many librarians are socially acquainted with the campus faculty. Why not ask these individuals to participate in a planned activity? A second good point of contact is through shared committee responsibilities. Librarians often serve on college and university committees and are in direct contact with the faculty. Another group that could be approached consists of those faculty members involved in collection development. Their activities show an overt interest in what is happening in the library, and they should be a good group to draw upon.

The type of bibliographic activities offered to any of the faculty could be varied. Some members of the faculty should be asked to bring their classes in for course-related lectures. Others are sorely in need of expert advice about the library assignment they have developed. Others may want to integrate a library unit that requires the students to look at a slide-tape program or videotape about using the library to do research. No matter what instructional activities are offered, it doesn't take long for information to spread to others on the faculty. Pleased faculty members pass on the good tidings to their colleagues, and soon the program is humming along with sufficient faculty support.

PERSONNEL SUPPORT

Beyond administrative and campus support, there is the question of whether there is enough personnel within the library to carry on instructional activities. It is difficult, if not impossible, for one individual to carry on more than a minimal instructional program. There must be an accurate count and a clear understanding about who will be participating. Here are some specific examples of the need for staff support. If guided orientation tours are offered, who will participate? Catalogers and other technical service librarians? Only public service librarians? Paraprofessionals, student help, other staff? If credit or course-related instruction is to be offered, are there librarians qualified and willing to teach? Are there any understood or written policies regarding public and/or technical service librarians' participation in instruction? Do librarians have the choice of not becoming involved with such activities? Is clerical support available to type, copy, and collate appropriate materials?

In trying to determine potential staff to participate in instructional activities, individuals should be asked to join the efforts being made. If some are hesitant because of insufficient experience, plans can be made for in-house training sessions. Also, opportunities to observe others teaching or giving tours will help to establish confidence. For those reluctant to work directly with the public, there is always work to be done on the handbook, bookmarks, slide-tape programs, or self-guided tours.

The best guideline that can be given is to let the program grow with the staff available. If there is minimal support, activities must be kept to a minimum. If there is widespread backing, more elaborate programs can be planned and developed. Individuals should not put themselves into that frustrating position of Sisyphus and try to carry the load alone. Be realistic and do what you can with the staff available.

THE ROLE OF PROGRAM GOALS AND OBJECTIVES

At some point in the planning process there must be decisions made about what direction a library's bibliographic program will take. These decisions, when formalized, become the program goals and objectives. Since there is not universal agreement on the various definitions of these terms, the following will be used for purposes of discussion:

---

1. PROGRAM GOALS:

   These are broad statements of content which are generally *not* measurable. They define the conditions to be achieved if the program is to be successful.

   EXAMPLES:

   A. To provide a successful library experience to the user.
   B. To acquaint the beginning library user with the physical layout of the library.

2. SPECIFIC PROGRAM OBJECTIVES:

   These are statements which describe the means to be used in achieving various goals. Well-written objectives include three parts (1) the action to be taken; (2) the criteria that will indicate that the objective has been met, and (3) a time frame.

   EXAMPLES:

   A. By the beginning of fall semester, a printed self-guided tour of the library will be made available at the library entrance.
   B. By June 198_, the instructional program will be included in the library budget as a separate item.

3. INSTRUCTIONAL OBJECTIVES:

   These are statements that indicate what the library user is expected to learn or achieve. These objectives are measurable and written in terms of the behavior expected from the library user. Instructional objectives are also known as behavioral objectives or enabling objectives.

   EXAMPLES:

   A. After completing a self-guided tour of the library, the library user will be able to locate the circulation desk and the reserve reading room without asking directions.
   B. Given the title of a magazine or journal, the library user will be able to independently use the serial listing system and retrieve the issue needed.

The process of writing goals and objectives is directly connected with the information that has been gathered about the library and its academic community. For goals and objectives to be viable, they must be based upon realistic needs and resources. If, for example, it is discovered that research papers are required in many of the education and psychology classes, program objectives should reflect this fact. Possible objectives could include that "the library will offer seminars covering the resources in education and psychology," or that "the library will offer a one-credit course on doing research in education and psychology." A third objective might indicate that "a slide-tape program or videotape on doing research in education and psychology will be made available to all classroom instructors in these areas." A library wouldn't offer all possible alternatives, but would choose to develop one or two that meet the needs of the students and the resources of the library.

Such specific program objectives can be written for all of the needs uncovered. For the basic-skills students, a program objective might include "a special unit on library skills to be integrated with the overall basic-skills program." For the graduate students, "a series of seminars in a particular discipline will be offered every fall [winter, spring] term." For the general student body, "term paper clinics will be offered on a weekly basis beginning with the fourth week of the term." There are any number of possibilities.

For those who are neophytes at writing goals and objectives, the following books will be helpful: *Writing Worthwhile Behavioral Objectives,* by Julie Vargas[3], and *Preparing Instructional Objectives,* by Robert Mager[4]. The ACRL's "Guidelines for Bibliographic Instruction in Academic Libraries,"[5] and the model statement of objectives in "Toward Guidelines for Bibliographic Instruction in Academic Libraries,"[6] should also prove useful to anyone at this stage of instructional program planning.

Setting Instructional Program Goals

Specific program goals should be set by those who have a vested interest in the instructional program. The more individuals and departments involved, the greater the need for group participation in this process. It is a serious mistake for one individual to unilaterally draw up the library's instructional goals and objectives. This is especially true if that individual must depend upon the cooperation of other areas of the library.

A library-wide committee that includes key members of various units and departments is recommended. At least one member of this group should represent the administration. Such a committee serves as an interdepartmental forum where problems and constraints can be discussed openly. It is this same committee that can be given the responsibility for setting the specific program goals and objectives. Mutual agreement by a library-wide group adds strength to the final document and avoids the criticism that instruction is being "imposed" by a small minority.

PATTERNS OF ADMINISTRATIVE STRUCTURE

Of vital importance to any bibliographic instructional program is its administrative structure. In discussing this point, the proverbial "chicken or egg" controversy arises. Should administrative structure be chosen to fit the activities planned, or should the administrative structure dictate the activities? Proponents of either side of the issue can present strong arguments. Generally, most academic libraries have superimposed some type of structure on existing instructional activities. However, no matter which direction is chosen, the following general comments about administrative structure are appropriate.

Minimal structure is usually found in libraries where there are one or two individuals who are committed to the concept of library instruction and have developed activities that they organize and administer. The existence of such programs is totally dependent on the willingness and availability of these individuals and very often fades into oblivion when interested parties leave. Often, their involvement with instruction is not recognized as part of their primary job responsibilities, and instruction becomes an "overload." In such cases, the library administration is not actively committed to the concept of library instruction and does little to support or advance it. Realistically, a balanced, vital instructional program cannot exist within such a structure.

A second type of structure involves administering the instructional program through an already existing department or section. Responsibility for the program may be delegated to one member of the department, rotated on a regular basis, or left with the department head. In smaller libraries or libraries with centralized services, this type of administrative structure works well. A strong program can be developed and the department or section is there to provide the necessary continuity. A variety of activities can be planned knowing there is personnel available. Responsibilities for such projects as orientation tours, handbooks, or printed guides can be shared.

In some libraries, committees play a significant part in the instructional program. Some are advisory and others are administrative. These committees are often instrumental in policy decisions and program planning. They review programs and make recommendations. Ad hoc committees are often formed to work on specific projects such as handbooks, slide-type programs, and staff-training seminars. However, even with such committees within a library, there should be one individual responsible for the day-to-day functioning of the program.

For the larger academic library and for libraries with decentralized services, departmental or committee administration of instruction is normally not sufficient. There is a need for a separate office to coordinate the instructional activities of the entire library. The emphasis here is on the word coordinate. The person in this position cannot carry out an entire instructional program either alone or with minimal staff. It is only through library-wide cooperation that well-balanced programs can be initiated and maintained.

What should such coordination involve? One of the best

descriptions of the purposes and responsibilities of such a position is found in the sample job description that Dyson included as part of a study he completed.

> The Library Instruction Coordinator, under the general direction of the Assistant Director for Public Services, is responsible for the initiation, development, and evaluation of a coordinated program of library instruction. He/she is responsible for keeping abreast of the latest developments in library instruction including audio-visual innovations and for making recommendations to improve the library's orientation and instructional programs.
>
> 1. The coordinator is primarily responsible for providing orientation and instruction to lower division undergraduates. Typical activities include:
>   a. Participating in campus-wide orientation programs for new students;
>   b. Preparing library guides, self-guided tours, and other aids to general library orientation for the main and branch libraries;
>   c. Acting as an advocate of bibliographic instruction, and working with faculty to integrate such instruction into classes; and
>   d. Acting as course coordinator for and teaching a section of the non-specialized credit course in bibliographic research.
> 2. The coordinator assists with upper-division and graduate-level instruction through:
>   a. Acting as a contact person for faculty and putting them in touch with the appropriate librarian;
>   b. Serving as a resource person to the reference and subject librarians providing such instruction;
>   c. Assisting with the selection and preparation of classroom materials (including teaching aids) for such instruction; and
>   d. Serving as a back-up instructor.
> 3. The coordinator regularly works some hours at major service points in the system, including the Main and Undergraduate Library reference desks.
> 4. The coordinator has the following administrative responsibilities:
>   a. Collect and organize statistics on library instruction in the library system;

b. Prepare an annual report on orientation/instructional activities within the system;
c. Train and supervise staff assigned to the instructional office;
d. Sit *ex officio* on the Library Instruction Advisory Committee; and
e. Participate in other library and university committee work as appropriate.[7]

Some libraries vary the above structure by providing the coordinator with an instructional staff. These individuals, who report directly to the coordinator, form what is basically a teaching department. Their primary responsibility is instruction—course-related instruction, tours, credit instruction, the preparation of printed guides, audiovisual material, etc. All or most instruction is conducted by this department and there is little involvement by librarians from other areas of the library.

In at least one library, Sangamon State, the entire library has been organized as a teaching library, with other duties, such as cataloging, acquisitions, and circulation, absorbed by qualified nonprofessionals. For a description of this system, which must be the ultimate in organizing for library instruction, Howard W. Dillon's article is recommended.[8]

Having some type of structure is essential. Leaving such an activity to chance or the whims of a few will most often result in weak and ineffective programming. Instruction, like acquisitions, cataloging, and circulation, should be appropriately organized and administered. Like these other activities, there isn't one "best" way. The needs and resources of each individual library determine the choice to be made.

PROGRAM DETAILS

Whatever the overall administrative structure, there are a number of general concerns that should be considered by anyone involved with an instructional program. First, there should be a readily identifiable point of contact for instructional activities. This normally means a telephone number, possibly a separate office, and identification of the individual responsible for program coordination. Many libraries use the general telephone number for the Undergraduate Library or the Reference Room. If there is a separate instructional office with its own telephone number, that office should be staffed so that incoming calls will be received and handled effectively. Separate offices with only part-time staff can cause much frustration for those trying to reach the contact person.

Whoever answers the phone should know the established procedures for accepting requests for such various activities as course-related classes or tours. That person should also be able to answer questions about the various aspects of the instructional program, or refer the caller to a person who may be able to help. It is helpful to have an instructional activities request form. This form, available at the service desk or in the appropriate office, should outline the information desired. This could include the name, address, and telephone number of the requester; activity desired; size of class or group; date preferred; time of day; and space for additional information such as special requests or a description of the library assignment. The appropriate person, such as the coordinator, should receive this request immediately so that action on the activity can be taken at once. The librarian assigned to the activity should confirm all arrangements with the requester as soon as possible, if this has not already been done by the coordinator.

A systematic method for assigning instructional requests should be established. The method chosen will depend on the structure of the program. If there is an identifiable instructional staff, requests can be handled routinely as part of the day-to-day assignments. If librarians from a number of departments are involved in instruction, there must be a procedure for clearing the assignment of instructional activities with both the librarian and the appropriate supervisor. In this type of situation, particularly in large libraries, it may be helpful to have a file of participating librarians which includes information on special areas of interest and exper-

Today's Date ______________

Date Requested (if any) ______________ Period ____________

Professor's Name ____________________________

Class Name & No. ______________ Size of Class ___________

Phone _________________

Comments:

Instruction Request Form

tise, and the amount of time available for instruction. Such a list should be updated at regular intervals and information should be gathered from new librarians.

Keeping Statistics

Statistics from past years can be helpful in planning and scheduling future assignments. Information about the various instructional activities should be kept and tabulated. These data could include the names of the course or groups, type of activity, name of faculty member, size of group, librarian assigned, and so forth. A sample statistics sheet is shown below. Such statistics sheets can provide basic information for analyzing instructional patterns. Professor X seems to bring in Class Y every term; therefore, it is anticipated that Professor X will be in again this coming term. The local high school debating club always requests a tour in the spring. Someone can be assigned to this group before its members call or write.

If instructional activities such as guided tours and course-related/integrated sessions can be anticipated, instructional assignments can be made at the beginning of a term or

BIBLIOGRAPHIC INSTRUCTION STATISTICS

TERM: ____________

DEPARTMENT: ____________

	Type**	Date	Name of Library Staff member	Name of Course	Name of Course Instructor	Number of Participants	Presentation Time	Additional Comments (equipment used; handouts, etc.)
1.								
2.								
3.								
4.								
5.								
6.								
7.								
8.								
9.								
10.								
11.								
12.								

**TYPE OF ACTIVITY CODE
1 - guided tour 2 - seminar 3 - class room lecture 4 - credit course 5 - other (specify in comment column)

INSTRUCTIONS: Fill in the appropriate columns for your activity. Some will apply; others will not. Completed sheets are due in the coordinator's office on the last day of the term.

semester. Librarians can then make contacts early and begin to plan their sessions with the course instructors.

Statistics on guided tours are also important. Which times are the busiest? Is the evening tour well attended? There may be a need for three tour guides at 1:00 P.M. and only one at 9:00 A.M. Maybe the tours should be scheduled at fifteen-minute intervals instead of on the hour. Over a period of time such statistics form a healthy basis for decisions about the instructional activities.

Publicity

Another major concern in the administration of instructional programs is publicity. How should various programs be advertised? Who is the intended audience? What is the least expensive and most effective means of reaching the largest number of potential users? Approaches will differ depending on the nature of the program and its intended audience.

Faculty can be alerted to the opportunities for library instruction through faculty tours, seminar announcements in a campus newsletter, interaction with a librarian on a committee, by another faculty member, or by a memo or phone call from a librarian. Students may be informed of services through posters, flyers, announcements in the student publications, bookmarks, and radio and/or TV announcements. Encouraging the faculty to announce special activities, such as graduate seminars, to their classes can be helpful.

Whatever types of publicity are utilized, someone must be in charge. This is normally the task of the coordinator. Other personnel may be engaged to make the posters, type the flyers, and prepare articles for the local newspaper, but a centralized office helps to unify the efforts and prevent the inadvertent release of inaccurate or conflicting information.

Classroom and Equipment

The management of audiovisual equipment and classroom space is another administrative responsibility of the instructional librarian. There should be a method for reserving equipment and/or classroom space. For a library with its own classrooms and equipment, it is relatively easy to set up a reservation procedure. A detailed, day-by-day calendar can be used effectively. Any individual planning an instructional activity can sign up on a first-come, first-served basis, and schedule conflicts can be resolved internally. Again, one centralized point for this is most efficient.

For those libraries that are dependent on a campus scheduling office, the procedure for reserving a room should be clearly understood. One person can be delegated the responsibility for making the arrangements and keeping a record of the dates and times that the various rooms have been reserved.

Similarly, if a library orders AV equipment through a campus-wide audiovisual service, there should be an understanding of the policies of the service. How many days ahead must the equipment be reserved? Will it be delivered? Picked up? Will someone run the machines? Can it be reserved for an extra day? Centralizing the request point and having the equipment delivered to one particular area of the library will make it easy for everyone involved. The possibility of borrowing the equipment for a full term should be pursued. This will obviously help in the scheduling process.

If one individual is responsible for the equipment arrangement, this person should also be notified about equipment breakdown. Repairs should be made as soon as possible. Inoperative equipment is virtually worthless. Some repairs, such as the replacement of a bulb, can be handled by a staff member. Major repairs may have to be sent out. The entire question of equipment will be discussed in more detail in a later chapter.

SOME FINAL WORDS

Instructional programs can be complex. There are many different factors that make up the total program, and the more organized these activities, the smoother the program's operation. Without the attention to the details involved in such programs, the day-to-day activities can be cumbersome and at times frustrating. Faculty, students, and staff can be quickly turned off by inefficient modes of operation. Developing a structure that is able to administer a program well is essential.

There isn't one ideal structure for all libraries. The type of program structure chosen should fit the needs of the library as well as those of the academic community. The individuals who administer the instructional program must be prepared to handle the many pressures involved and also be constantly alert to the factors, internal and external, that can affect the program.

FOOTNOTES

1. John Lubans, Jr., "Evaluating Library-User Education Programs," in John Lubans, Jr., ed., *Educating the Library User* (New York: Bowker, 1974), p. 232.
2. The University of Texas at Austin Libraries, *A Comprehensive Program of User Education for The General Libraries* (ERIC Educational Document Reproduction Service, ED 148 401, 1977), 115 pp.
3. Julie S. Vargas, *Writing Worthwhile Behavioral Objectives* (New York: Harper & Row, 1972).
4. Robert F. Mager, *Preparing Instructional Objectives* (2nd ed.; Belmont, Cal.: Fearon Publishers, 1975).
5. "Guidelines for Bibliographic Instruction in Academic Libraries," *College and Research Libraries News* 38:92 (April 1977).
6. "Toward Guidelines for Bibliographic Instruction in Academic Libraries," *College and Research Libraries News* 36:137-139+ (May 1975).
7. Allan J. Dyson, "Organizing Undergraduate Library Instruction: The English and American Experience," *Journal of Academic Librarianship* 1:9-13 (March 1975). Also ERIC Educational Document Reproduction Service, ED 152 308.
8. Howard W. Dillon, "Organizing the Academic Library for Instruction," *Journal of Academic Librarianship* 1:4-7 (March 1975).

SUGGESTED READINGS

Dyson, Allan J. "Organizing Undergraduate Library Instruction: The English and American Experience." *Journal of Academic Librarianship* 1 (March 1975): 9-13.

Fjallbrant, Nancy. "Planning a Programme of Library User Education." *Journal of Librarianship* 9 (July 1977): 199-211.

Lubans, John, Jr. "Objectives for Library-Use Instruction in Educational Curricula," in John Lubans, Jr., ed., *Educating the Library User,* pp. 211-220. New York: Bowker, 1974.

The University of Texas at Austin General Libraries. *A Comprehensive Program of User Education for The General Libraries.* ERIC Educational Document Reproduction Service, 1977. 115 pp. ED 148 401.

The University of Wisconsin-Parkside University Libraries. *Bibliographic Instruction Program.* ERIC Educational Document Reproduction Service, 1976. 62 pp. ED 126 937.

Wood, D. N. "Discovering the User and His Information Needs." *ASLIB Proceedings* 21 (July 1969): 262-270.

CHAPTER 2

Orientation

The term "library orientation" is not new. In fact, historically this expression has been used to describe any attempt at instructing students in the ways and means of using a library. In recent years, however, orientation has taken on a special, more limited meaning of its own. It is that portion of library instruction which introduces patrons to the physical layout of a library, and has become but one aspect of library instruction. The whole question of providing orientation to library patrons has become a controversial issue among instructional librarians. Some libraries consider orientation unnecessary and have dropped their orientation activities. Unless the library is completely self-explanatory when one enters the building, this seems to be an unwise decision. Although it is easy for librarians and library staff to forget what it is like to enter a strange building, and although they seem to be tempted to save instructional efforts for credit or course-related classes, there are always students and faculty new to the library.

With this in mind, orientation activities should be kept and used as the beginning step to a larger, more involved instructional program. Many students and faculty may not have the opportunity to take a credit course in library skills. Also, not every class is scheduled for course-related library sessions. Continuing education students should not be forgotten. They frequently use the library during the evening and weekend hours. In addition to the service being provided to the patrons, orientation can also serve to reduce the number of directional questions that often plague the library staff. Library orientation is a sound concept and it should be available in one form or other.

The chief means of library orientation is usually a library tour, although handbooks, open houses, and signs all have a role to play. Even though the concept of the library tour seems simple, there are many varieties of touring methods, ranging from the traditional guided tour, to self-guided tours, audio tours, and stationary video tours. Each of these methods has advantages and disadvantages and the most appropriate choice will depend upon the nature of the library, the audience for whom the tour is intended, and the personal preference of the librarian. A one-room library presents different problems than a sprawling structure with added wings, annexes, or decentralized services. Many libraries find it advantageous to offer more than one type of tour. It is the aim of this chapter to discuss the varieties of tours, guidelines for developing each, and such matters as coordination with other campus programs, handling special groups, and arranging open houses.

THE PRINTED SELF-GUIDED TOUR

Self-guided tours allow patrons to initiate their own tours whenever the library is open. Visitors, students, and faculty are not forced to wait for a particular day or time for scheduled guided tours. Self-guided tours are especially useful in meeting the needs of the evening or weekend students who are not able to come to the library during the day.

The most common form for the self-guided tour is a printed handout. This comes in all sizes, colors, and prints. Some are completely developed and printed in-house. Others are very sophisticated and make use of professional graphics. Whatever the process, the handout should be attractive and accurate. This material is usually the first con-

Coláiste Mhuire Gan Smál Luimneach 94586

Reprinted with permission of the

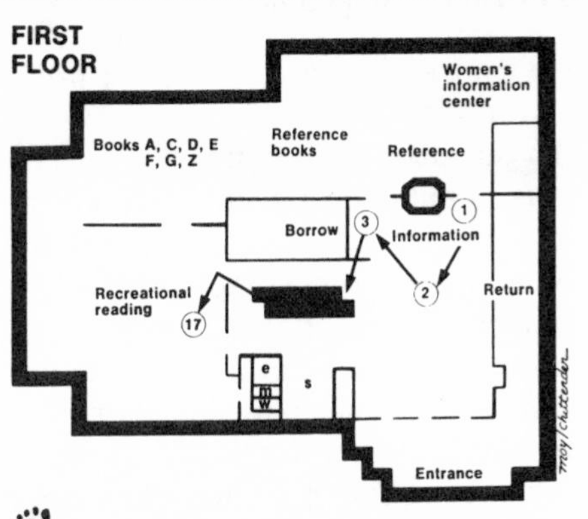

1. INFORMATION-REFERENCE SERVICE

This is where you begin when you don't know how to begin work on a project. Librarians will help you find quick factual information, general campus information, show you how to use library resources and assist in planning your research strategy. Appointments for consultation are also available.

To the right is the card catalog which lists books and nonprint media owned by this library. For more information about the card catalog, take a brochure in the holder near footprint #1. Note at the desk the "Serials List" which is a computer printout listing magazines and newspapers held by the campus library system.

Reference books and periodical indexes are shelved in the area beyond the desk. Information and Occupational Files are located to the left of the Information Desk. These consist of pamphlet materials on many topics and occupations arranged by subject which are *not* listed in the card catalog.

(to find step 2, go toward the center of the lobby near the escalators)

2. LOBBY

The lobby areas on all five floors of this building are similar. In each lobby area you will find drinking fountains, public and campus phones, bulletin boards, and floor

Undergraduate Library, University of Maryland.

tact the patron will have with the library. An inferior product should be avoided at all costs.

There are many ways to put together a printed tour. The samples included with this chapter will help to illustrate this point. There are, however, some common elements included in most printed tours. The first is a map of the building or a layout of the various floors of the library. Such graphics serve as road maps and they help to guide the patrons from one area to another. Another part of the printed tour is some type of number or letter coding that is keyed to explanatory material. This information provides specific details about the various areas being visited. Sometimes, if a building is extremely complicated, it is necessary to provide very detailed directions. Such directions may say to "take the stairwell on the left" or "continue to walk down the hall and enter the west wing." In addition to the features just mentioned, many libraries use the printed tours for the inclusion of extra information. This might include a list of other campus libraries, policies on smoking or food, and specifics about copy machines, lockers, group studies, and carrels.

For anyone interested in developing a printed tour, it is most helpful to examine as many different samples of tours as possible from other libraries. In addition to the ones included here, Project LOEX has a good collection that can be borrowed. Also, some state clearinghouses may have samples of printed tours available.

Developing the Printed Self-guided Tour

Developing a printed self-guided tour for a library is not a "mission impossible." In fact, it can be a rewarding experience. Here are some key steps in developing such a tour:

STEP 1 Decide whether your library needs this type of tour by asking yourself the following questions: (a) Is your library large or complex enough to warrant a printed tour? (b) What audience will this help (continuing education, evening classes, general public . . .)? (c) Will this replace or supplement an existing program? (d) Can it be used with specific classes as an aid to instruction? (e) Will the patrons make use of it? (f) How much will it cost (include overhead and staff time)?

STEP 2 Consult, as appropriate, with administrators and/or committees. If you have completed step 1, you should have strong arguments for adoption of the project. You should be prepared for some ball-park figures on cost, staff time, intended production schedule, and so on. Be as open as possible to all discussion and suggestions. Remember, projects such as this need administrative support to be successful.

STEP 3 Decide what areas are important enough to be included in the tour.

STEP 4 Obtain floor plans. Look for previous handbooks or in-house publications that may include a map. An office may have blueprints or schematic drawings that may be of help. Many printed tours have very simple floor plans which have been drawn by the person developing the tour.

STEP 5 Write a description for each area of the library you are coding. Try to keep it simple. Consult with staff in the various areas. They can check the accuracy of the statements and may be able to make suggestions for improvement.

STEP 6 Decide upon a logical pattern to be followed. Try out the projected route, making adjustments as necessary.

STEP 7 Code numbers or letters may need to be posted in the various areas. Such signs may be hand-made or ordered through a graphic service. Press-on letters work well and look professional. Until the "bugs" are worked out, it is not wise to invest in anything permanent. The codes should be large enough to read and should be posted in prominent places.

STEP 8 Code the map and the explanations.

STEP 9 Take the tour again, using the map and explanation. Write out the directions necessary for directing a person from one area to another. Some imaginative libraries have used color-coded floor stripes, and at least one library has painted footsteps on the floor to aid in the process.

STEP 10 Try out your "final" product on a few willing subjects. Revise any weak or faulty portions which are uncovered.

STEP 11 Check with a printer and make arrangements for printing the guide. Try to keep the graphics uncluttered, the product eye-catching and attractive. (This is where samples from other libraries may help.)

STEP 12 Put the finished product in an obvious place (entrance, lobby, etc.). You may wish to attach an informal questionnaire to the first set printed. A drop box at your last number will provide a convenient place for users to leave their comments and the printed tour if they wish to do so.

STEP 13 Before ordering a second printing, revise any weak areas uncovered by observation or the questionnaires. Check with the staff in the various areas for their input.

STEP 14 "Fait accompli." Keep an eye on your supply. Check to see that your coding is not missing from any area. Watch for sections which may need updating. Notifying you of changes is usually the last thing busy supervisors think of when they are rearranging a section of the library. Keeping your tour up-to-date is no small responsibility

---

THE AUDIO SELF-GUIDED TOUR

The audio tour is commonly encountered by the public in places such as museums or art galleries and is often quite effective. Some academic libraries have successfully adapted this technique for their orientation program. Audio tours involve the use of a portable tape player, a tape, and a headphone. An individual is able to listen to audio explanations of various areas of the library while walking through the building. A printed handout (usually a map or floor plan) is often available with the tour. This type of tour can be provided on demand, and provides flexibility to an orientation program.

The audio tour is a more sophisticated endeavor than the printed self-guided tour. There are many details that should be closely examined before heading in this direction. The most obvious consideration is the cost of establishing such a program. The initial investment involves the purchase of a sufficient number of tape players, headphones, and tapes to meet the anticipated demand. According to the latest figures, portable tape players range in price from $30 to $60 and may be purchased from commercial companies. These prices are dependent on what features the players have. The cost of headphones varies from just under $10 to $25. Can your library afford such a program?

The next major consideration is the housing and availability of the AV equipment and tapes. Making such equipment self-service is not advisable as it opens the door for theft. The equipment may have to be distributed through an office or service area. Obvious candidates for a distribution point are the circulation area, information/reference areas, or some office readily accessible from the entrance. More staff may be a necessity if this added activity could not be absorbed by such areas.

Finally, consideration must be given to equipment maintenance. This would include general cleaning, battery changes, equipment repairs, overhauls, and dubbing of new tapes. The cost of a service contract should also be examined. It may be necessary to hire new staff to complete the above activities on a regular basis.

Developing the Audio Tour

Almost all the steps described for developing the printed self-guided tour are necessary and appropriate. Remember, however, that it is necessary to write a "script" to be read and recorded by an individual. This script should be conversational in nature, yet must also provide the basic facts. The tour should be "paced," allowing enough time for patrons to walk from one area to another. It may be advisable to work directly with a person in the AV department, who should have good technical advice to offer. Borrowing samples of

McKISSICK MEMORIAL LIBRARY

Self-Guided Tour and General Information

The University of South Carolina

Reprinted with permission of the University of South Carolina. Note: the Cooper Library was opened.

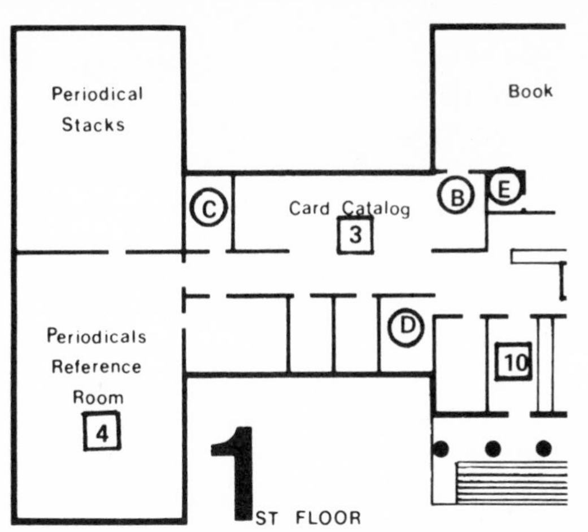

SELF-GUIDED TOUR

1. **ENTRANCE.** Exhibits of special interest, usually notable materials from the Library's collections, are kept in the glass cases to your left.

2. **CIRCULATION DESK.** All circulating materials in McKissick are checked out here for use outside of the library. A current, validated University I-D card is required. It is not necessary to fill out a charge slip for books entered on the Automated Circulation System, identified by the Library Number label inside the front cover. The loan period is three weeks. Books may not be renewed by phone. Fines for overdue books are 10 cents a day.

To the right of the Circulation Desk is an IBM copier, coin-operated at 5 cents a copy.

To the left of the Circulation Desk is the Card Catalog.

3. **CARD CATALOG.** This is a union catalog, listing by author, title, and subject, books in all campus libraries. It does not include most periodicals and U.S. governemnt publications, which are indexed elsewhere. Materials not in McKissick are indicated by a special location symbol above the call number; notice the Special Location Chart on the East wall of the area for an explanation of these symbols. The Stack Location chart, giving locations for materials in

McKissick Memorial Library ceased to exist in 1976 when the Thomas audio tours may also be of some help. A very good source of information is an article by Millicent Palmer, "Creating Slide-Tape Library Instruction: The Librarian's Role."[1]

It may be necessary to have some type of printed material available. First, patrons will need instruction on operating the equipment. This may be done verbally by someone at the service desk, through posted signs, or possibly through directions attached to the equipment. A map or floor plan is often a necessary supplement. This can make a nice handout, especially if library hours, loan periods, and important phone numbers are included somewhere on the sheet.

In summary, audio tours are generally more expensive than other types of orientation tours. There is a need for special equipment and special handling of the equipment. Such tours do provide a flexibility that is not provided by guided tours, and can be a valuable part of an orientation program.

STATIONARY AUDIOVISUAL PROGRAMS

A spin-off from the self-guided tour has been the stationary orientation program. This involves the use of some type of audio and visual material set up in a permanent place in the library. The most common type of stationary program consists of a slide/tape combination, although videotape and 8mm film are also used.

It is necessary to develop the equivalent of a tour using audio and visual material. Advances in AV technology enable the program to run continuously or to play through once, stop, and then begin again when someone activates the system. This equipment and software are usually placed in a location near the library entrance. They should be protected from tampering, and it may be necessary to provide a protective cabinet to house the equipment. Sometimes handouts are available nearby. Patrons are now able to receive an overview of the library without actually taking a walk. This type of set-up can be an excellent supplement to other orientation activities.

THE GUIDED TOUR

Requiring less time to prepare than self-guided tours, the traditional guided tour is probably the most common form of library orientation. It has in its favor the direct contact of the public with library staff who can respond to questions and other expressions of interest, puzzlement, or boredom. The guided tour can be tailored to fit the needs of various groups, from freshmen to faculty to visiting alumni. It can be varied on the spur of the moment, unlike the printed or taped tour.

The tour usually involves meeting the group at a prearranged spot such as the main entrance of the library or the reference area. The group is then taken through the building, with brief stops at various points, where basic information about the library is given. Discussions would include the card catalog, the arrangement of the stacks, periodical indexes and collections, reference services, book-borrowing procedures, and library hours. Its concern is with where things are and what services are offered. The details are best left for later.

With careful planning the guided tour can be an excellent means of doing what it is intended to do: introduce the patron to the library. Carefully thought-out goals and objectives, well-planned routes, proper pacing and scheduling, and thorough preparation of tour leaders will all contribute to successful guided tours.

The first step is to clarify the goals and objectives of the tour. These will vary according to the group for which the tour is planned. The general goal will be to acquaint the patron with the physical layout of the library, including the location of essential services. There may also be affective goals, such as developing good feelings about the library and arousing curiosity. Tours for freshmen may stress the classification system, the arrangement of the card catalog, the location of periodicals and indexes, library hours, the reserve system, and circulation policies. A graduate student tour may dwell on special subject reference areas, interlibrary loans, or the availability of carrel assignments. For faculty members you may wish to emphasize instructional services, reserve regulations, faculty privileges, and the names of people to contact for specialized information on matters such as acquisitions or library instruction. For alumni you may wish to emphasize new additions to the building, archival collections, or memorabilia.

With all groups, concentrate on the basic essentials. Avoid too much detail, and liven up your tour with some interesting stories or tidbits of information. Give tips on how to find things. Make people feel they are getting some "inside secrets" that make the tour worthwhile. Have a ready supply of interesting topical examples of what they might look up in the card catalog or a periodical index. Are there any library traditions, ghost tales, or funny stories? What happens if you go through the electronic detection system with a hidden book? What kinds of questions do people ask at the reference desk? What are some surprising items the library user can locate in the documents collection?

In the final analysis you must decide what your students need, what your library needs, and what kind of image you wish to project. When you have completed your list of objectives and identified the areas to be emphasized on the tour, it is advisable to confer with the supervisors of the various areas. Seeking out these people is very important because hard feelings can develop if tour leaders blithely give out inaccurate information about a particular service or area, or if the information given does not include what the person in charge feels to be essential.

Once you have your list of objectives and your reports from various parts of the library, you can outline the progression of the tour from point to point. You may wish to type your plan in the form of tour notes—including your objectives for each area, followed by the information provided by each area. These notes can then be distributed to tour guides as part of their training. You may wish to have three or four alternate routes for your tour so that you could handle several groups at one time. You may wish to consider having groups meet in a lecture room, give them handouts, perhaps present a program utilizing audiovisual materials, and give them a brief explanation of where they will be going and what the purpose of the tour is before you lead them about. If you do not have facilities to do that, it is often a good idea to gather the group in a quiet spot at the beginning so that the tour leader can give some introductory information. The old axiom, "First you tell them what you're going to tell them, then you tell them, and then you tell them what you've just told them," works as well for the orientation tour as for other forms of public communication. If you can whet the group's interest in what is to come right at the beginning, you will be well on your way to preventing boredom.

Another factor in determing the tour's success is the size of the group. A tour with one or two can be a great success, but more than 15 in a group is difficult. Students often cannot see and hear in the larger groups, and such a group inevitably causes more disruption in the library. In addition, the larger the group, the longer the walking time. You may be able to practically jog your way through with two or three, but with 15, you begin to feel you're herding cattle.

It is often difficult to conduct a tour without creating a disturbance. Sometimes one can stop just outside the entrance to a room, do most of the explaining there, and then let the group walk through in silence. Be wary of blocking doorways and traffic flow. The group will follow you, so walk where you want everyone to stand and then circle back to them. Again, the smaller the group, the easier it is to be discreet.

It is a good idea to bring the students back to the starting point—usually the main entrance. Before dismissing the group, ask if there are any questions. Printed handouts such as bookmarks and handbooks can be distributed to the group. This material will serve as a review of the information given in the tour.

Staffing for Guided Tours

Many different staffing patterns may be used for orientation tours. Some libraries try to have all of the tours assigned to the professional staff. There are very good reasons for this approach. The librarians should be able to deliver accurate information about the library and its services. They are also able to present mini-instructional sessions while in areas such as the card catalog. They should be able to respond to detailed questions about various places such as circulation or reserve readings. Some libraries use only their public service librarians for tours. Others try to involve all members of the professional staff, including the technical operations personnel. The advantage of this latter approach is that the tours (often considerable in number) are shared by many and provide a feeling of involvement in the instructional program for all the library staff.

At some academic institutions students are used as tour guides. These are often upper-division students who work part time in the library. They can save on the investment of professional time in this activity, but there tends to be a loss of in-depth information. Another pattern uses a combination of professionals and "qualified" full-time or part-time staff. There are often many staff members who have the experience and knowledge to give excellent tours.

No matter which pattern is adopted, there is a need for training of the tour guides. This can take the form of a printed handout describing the various areas, or it may be advantageous to have a formal discussion session, particularly if student guides are used. Any policy changes or relocation projects should be noted and updated. It is a good idea for novice tour leaders to observe one or two tours by experienced leaders before they venture out on their own.

Handling Special Groups

Tours for special groups can be developed using the same kind of planning and consideration given to developing regular tours. You may wish to design a tour for foreign students with emphasis on some conventions and basic reference books with which they might not be familiar. Take extra care to speak clearly and carefully. You may wish to develop a tour for the handicapped which stresses routes around the library accessible by wheelchair, entrances for the handicapped, special services for the blind, and people to contact for assistance with particular problems. Sometimes tours are planned in conjunction with course-related instruction, in which case those areas pertinent to the field of study are emphasized. A tour is often helpful following an instructional session so that the exact locations of some of the materials discussed in class can be pointed out. An education class, for example, might be shown where the Library of Congress "L" classification books are shelved in the reference area and in the stacks, or where the most frequently used "Z" classification is found. One may wish to have tours for the Upward Bound, Developmental Year, or similar special student programs scheduled in conjunction with the coordinators of those programs. Knowing the library needs of the academic community is important in planning tours for special groups.

Policy Statements

Unfortunately, not all requests for tours are legitimate, and one finds it necessary to set some guidelines. It is good to have a policy statement specifying any groups for whom tours will or will not be given. You may decide, for example, to eliminate tours for elementary-school children, for scouting groups, and general high-school groups, if you find that they are taking too much of your time. The college or university may have policies regarding access to the library. These should be reviewed.

TOURS AS PART OF FRESHMAN ORIENTATION PROGRAMS

Many colleges have comprehensive freshmen and new-student orientation programs, some of which are voluntary, and some mandatory. Some programs operate before the terms begin or during the summer; others are offered throughout the school year. In planning library orientation programs it is wise to work closely with people involved in the overall orientation plan. Ideally, the student's introduction to the library should be carefully planned as part of the entire educational program. It will make a difference in your approach if the library tour is mandatory or voluntary. Although it is not always possible to make a choice between the two, there are some differences that should be considered.

A mandatory tour insures that students receive the same exposure to basic aspects of the library whether they think that they need to know them or not. It also means some students who would never go near the library of their own free will are led into it and may find that it is a place to which they would like to return.

The disadvantages of the mandatory tour are the large number of students often involved and the difficulty of arousing and sustaining the interest of a captive and often unwilling audience. It may be argued that unless the student has a need to know, most lecturing, touring, and teaching is useless. On the other hand, one may argue that only by being forcibly shown the intricacies and complexities of an academic library will the students have any idea of what they might yet have to learn to be academically successful. Your decision on the type of tour to be offered will depend partly on your philosophy, partly on the philosophy of the institution, and partly on the ever-changing trends in higher education.

OPEN HOUSES

The term "open house"is frequently heard in the field of sales. Realtors have open houses to sell homes. Businesses have open houses to feature their goods to a potential market. Since libraries are trying to "sell" their products and services to the public, an open house can be a valuable activity. During an open house the entire library is on display.

Exhibits are planned and arranged with eye-catching and interesting material. Tours are arranged at convenient times, and special talks or demonstrations, perhaps featuring highly interesting areas such as maps or rare books, are scheduled. Most open houses last all or part of the day, but such activities could be extended for a longer period of time. Some libraries plan their open house around a key event, such as the opening of the fall term, homecoming week, or National Library Week. The date and time should be chosen carefully with full consideration given to conflicting activities on campus or in the community. It can be quite discouraging to spend time and effort on an open house only to find that 90 percent of the campus population is involved in a concert or sports rally.

A most important ingredient for a successful open house is publicity. Posters, flyers, and media announcements should be visible and sent out well ahead of time. Local television and radio stations often provide free community announcements. However, they do require a certain amount of lead time. Student publications and campus bulletin boards are effective means of publicizing, and free handouts, such as book markers, balloons, or lapel buttons, add a festive air to the day and also serve as advertisements.

A well-planned open house can be a valuable activity, not only for the instructional program, but for the public relations of the library. It puts the library in the spotlight for a few hours and provides an opportunity for patrons to experience the library at its best. Making the academic community aware of the materials and services available in the library through an activity such as an open house is a worthy goal for any instructional program.

FINAL NOTE

Orientation activities are the backbone of library instructional programs. There are many different means of carrying out such activities; self-guided tours, audio tours, stationary audiovisual programs, guided tours, and open houses. Individuals involved in a library's instructional program must decide what is most effective for their patrons and their programs. This decision in turn should be based upon the time and money available to develop any one of the methods.

FOOTNOTES

1. Millicent Palmer, "Creating Slide-Tape Library Instruction: The Librarian's Role," *Drexel Library Quarterly* 8:251-267 (July 1972).

SUGGESTED READINGS

Foster, Barbara. "Do-It-Yourself Videotape for Library Orientation Based on a Term Paper Project." *Wilson Library Bulletin* (February 1974): 476-481.

Hughes, J. Marshal. "Tour of the Library by Audio-Tape." *Special Libraries* 65 (July 1974): 288-290.

Lynch, Mary Jo. "Library Tours: The First Step," in John Lubans, Jr., ed., *Educating the Library User*, pp. 254-268. New York: Bowker, 1974.

Palmer, Millicent. "Creating Slide-Tape Library Instruction: The Librarian's Role." *Drexel Library Quarterly* 8 (July 1972): 251-267.

Schramm, Jeanne and Stewart, Frances. "The Use of the Slide Presentation in Library Orientation," in Barbara Mertins, comp., *Bibliographic Instruction*, pp. 20-30. West Virginia Library Association. Working Conference of the College and University Section. ERIC Educational Document Reproduction Service, 1977. ED 144 582.

Schwartz, Philip John, comp. *The New Media in the Academic Library Orientation* 1950-1972: *An Annotated Bibliography*. ERIC Educational Document Reproduction Service, 1973. ED 071 682.

Sim, Yong Sup. *A Self-Guided Library Tour Method at Mercer County Community College. The Learning Theory and Applications Module*. ERIC Educational Document Reproduction Service, 1976. ED 135 342.

CHAPTER 3

The Printed Word: Handbooks, Bibliographies, Topical Guides, Miscellaneous Printed Guides, and Signs

INTRODUCTION

One of the great shocks that a newcomer to teaching receives is the discovery of the tremendous amount of time it takes. Several hours are often necessary to prepare for a single one-hour presentation. It is when librarians look at the time required for instruction that they frequently question whether it is all worth it. One way of conserving precious and expensive staff time is through the use of means other than person-to-person contact. In this chapter we will discuss some basic methods of instruction through the printed word: library handbooks, bibliographies, topical guides, miscellaneous printed guides, and signs.

Printed materials can meet needs filled by neither the

one-to-one assistance available at the reference desk nor formal instruction. They are frequently utilized by the casual library user and those patrons who need help but hesitate to "bother" anyone by asking. Such materials can introduce these individuals to many aspects of the library about which they would otherwise never know. By judicious use of the printed word, instruction can be provided with minimal use of staff time and at the same time the number of repetitious questions at the reference desks can be reduced.

According to British librarian Malcolm B. Stevenson, the first task of those involved in library instruction should be to make sure that the library systems employed "are effective, straightforward, and self-explanatory." He quotes Line and Tidmarsh, saying library instruction is all too often the "thread through an unnecessary labyrinth."[1] Making all library systems effective and self-explanatory undoubtedly goes beyond the scope of library instruction, but printed guides to these systems certainly bring together efforts to make the systems self-explanatory and instructive.

LIBRARY HANDBOOKS

There are probably as many types of library handbooks as there are libraries. They come in all sizes and formats—from booklets to single sheets designed to be used together or separately—and vary widely in the amount and type of information included. Nevertheless, the handbook is usually designed to provide the user with an introduction to a particular library. It may contain a floor plan or list identifiable areas of the building. It usually mentions services, policies, hours, rules, special collections, and sometimes personnel. It may give instruction on how to use the card catalog or how to locate serials, and it may or may not explain the library's classification system. Some handbooks are designed for specific audiences—undergraduates, graduates, or faculty—while most are aimed at all library users. Some libraries insert supplements for faculty or graduate students into their handbooks. Some refer the reader to other library publications which provide additional information on specific topics.

While most academic libraries have handbooks, there appears to have been little study of their effectiveness or use. With the rising cost of paper and printing, there is concern that they are simply "throwaways" which could be dispensed with. Nevertheless, patrons seem to feel a need for some printed material they can take with them and consult again. When one library was without a handbook for over a year, there were many requests for "just anything telling about the library."

The library handbook has many uses. It can serve as a reference for the library staff, especially newcomers, part-time, and student help. It can answer requests about the library's hours, circulation policies, and directions to the restrooms, telephones, photocopy machines, and coin changers. It provides a written statement of the library's policies and procedures which may be used to settle questions or challenges by the users. It can serve as a public relations device to impress visitors, alumni, and prospective students. It can set a welcoming tone which encourages faculty and students to make use of library services and facilities.

Planning the Contents of the Handbook

There is little in library literature that is truly helpful for designing a handbook. An exception is the U.S. Federal Library Committee's *Guidelines for Library Handbooks,*[2] an outstanding document which should be required reading for every handbook designer. Other useful but somewhat less specific articles are listed at the end of the chapter.

In the Foreward to the *Guidelines* the committee states that the purpose of a handbook is "to convey to the library user the scope, resources, and services of the library itself." The guidelines are brief and to the point, covering "Information to Be Included, Order of Presentation, Styles of Writing,

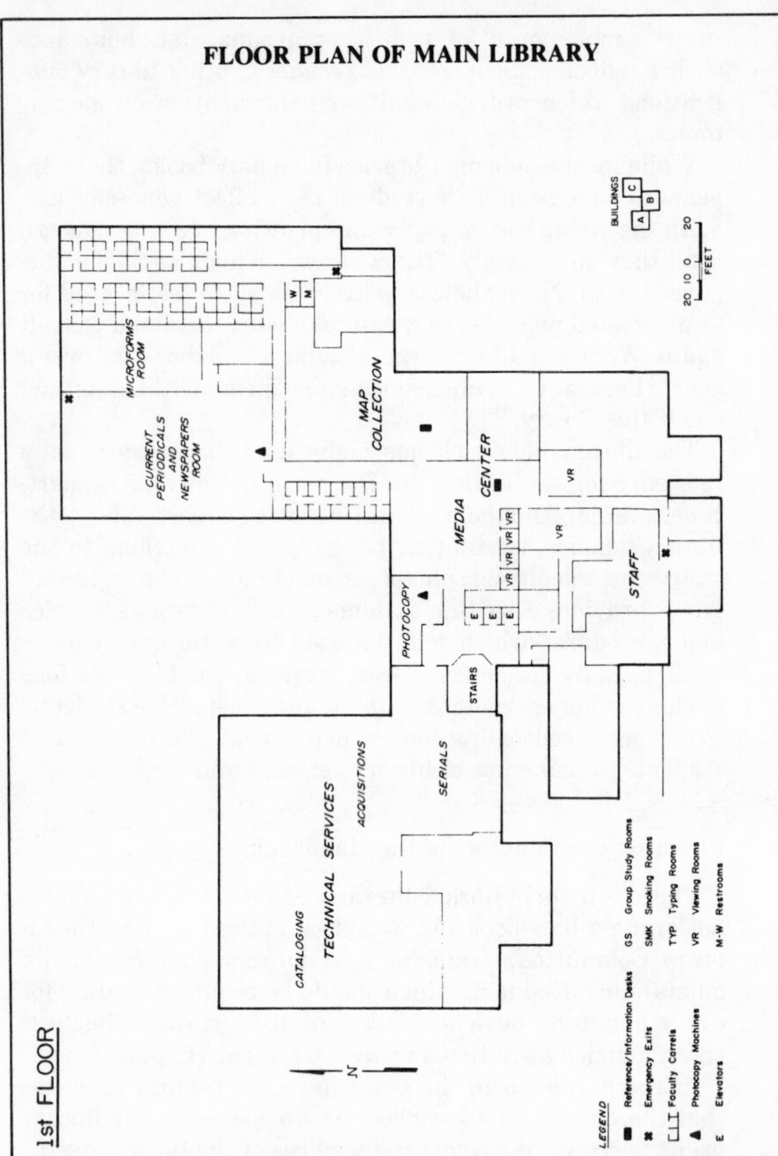

Floorplan of the main library of the University of Arizona reprinted with

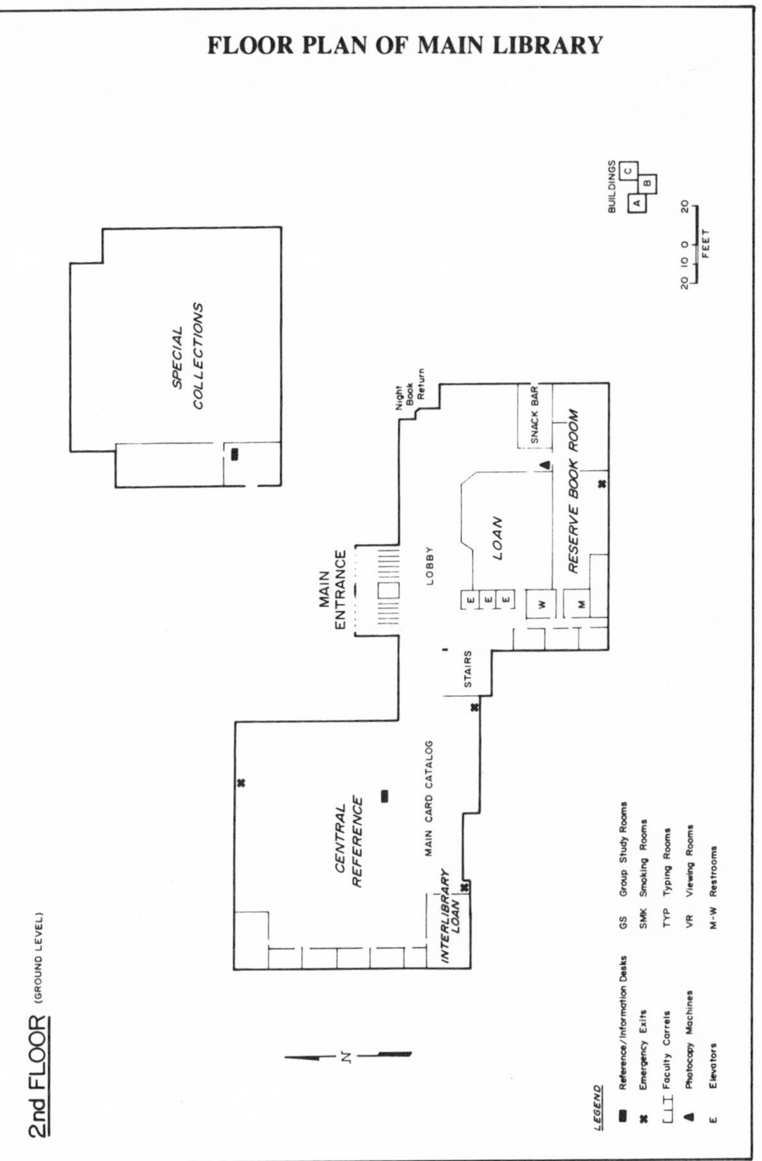

permission of the University of Arizona Library.

Format and Design (including page size, number of pages, type, illustrations, placement, paper and color.)" There is also a helpful list of supplementary readings on planning and producing any kind of printed material.

In planning a handbook it is important to think carefully about the kinds of information the users of your library need, and how this information can best be conveyed to them. A listing of most frequently asked questions at various service desks can provide a start. The Federal Committee's guidelines point out that the handbook should be written with the user's interests, not the librarian's, in mind. They suggest, for example, that headings read "How to Obtain a Book" or "Books: How to Obtain Them," rather than "Circulation" and "Interlibrary Loan," which are operations of major significance to the librarian, but probably not to the student.[3]

It is good to try out suggestions on students and faculty and ask what they feel needs to be included. After all, the handbook is for them, not for those who work in the library every day and are so accustomed to the idiosyncrasies of the building and its systems that these have become second nature to them.

Before the handbook is complete, staff members representing all departments and all levels, from clerks to division heads and directors, should be asked to review what has been written and make suggestions, especially for those sections concerning their areas. Many helpful comments may be gained and many potential pitfalls avoided. However, one must guard against a complete rewriting from the library staff's rather than the user's point of view, and against inclusion of detail that may be dear to a section supervisor, but unsuited to the scope and purposes of the handbook.

Who Should be Responsible?

In some libraries the responsibility for writing and revising the handbook is assigned to a member of the reference staff. In other libraries a handbook committee is drawn from various areas of the library. In yet others an administrative officer, a director of public relations, or a coordinator of instruction assumes responsibility. It may be wise to delegate the actual writing and editing to one or two people to avoid the blandness and monotony that tend to characterize committee-produced documents. This will also reduce the time-consuming discussion that inevitably occurs over matters of emphasis and style.

Distribution

There should also be a delegation of responsibility for distribution of the handbook. It must be decided whether it will be distributed to faculty and students individually, or whether it will be left on library service desks or in a display rack to be picked up by those who come into the building. Perhaps a member of the secretarial or clerical staff could be assigned to look after such details as keeping track of how fast copies are going and ordering replacements. It may be feasible to sell the handbook at bookstores or through vending machines, or to place a drop-off box near the building exit, where patrons who wish to do so can deposit their handbooks when they leave.

Revision

Plans for revisions of the handbook should also be considered during the planning stage. The date of publication should be included in the handbook, and the date of the next revision taken into consideration in deciding both the information to be included and the format of the book. Information that is likely to change could be presented in a way that will be easy to change. For example, library hours and circulation policies might be listed inside the front or back covers, so that only the cover need be reprinted. Such information could also be included as an insert. If the handbook is the responsibility of a committee, it is helpful to have one

The Georgetown University Library exists to serve the needs of our students and faculty. The library operates on an open-stack principle and most materials are available on a self-service basis. To assist the reader, floor plan diagrams and stack directories have been posted throughout the building. Library hours are posted in the third floor lobby.

FIRST FLOOR

Audiovisual Department The Audiovisual Department has a collection of spoken and music tapes, microforms, films, slides and video-tapes. Assistance in using the A/V card catalog and A/V materials is available at the Service Desk. Two group viewing rooms are available for classes using audiovisual materials.

Copying Services A staff-operated Xerox machine is available to students and faculty. This section can also make prints from microfilm and microfiche. A number of other photographic services are also available.

SECOND FLOOR

Periodicals Bound and current unbound periodicals are shelved in alphabetical order by title or sponsoring association. A list of periodicals owned by the Georgetown University Libraries and the *Consortium Union List of Serials* can be consulted at the Reference Desk and at the index table on the 2nd floor. Further assistance is available from the Periodical Information Office on the 3rd floor. Periodicals do not circulate to students. General and specialized indexes to periodical literature are available in the Reference Department.

Newspapers Current daily newspapers are located to the left of the periodicals. Weekly newspapers are interfiled with the periodicals. Newspaper holdings are listed in the periodical print-out. Newspapers on microfilm are kept in the Audiovisual Department.

Government Documents The library has been a selective depository for U. S. government documents since October 1969. Most documents published after 1969 are not listed in the card catalog, but will be located in this department.

Reprinted with permission of the Joseph Mark Lauinger Memorial Library,

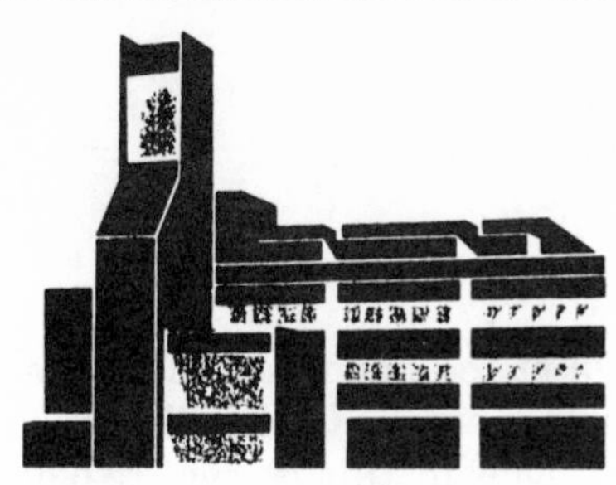

FLOOR	Books. Class L-Z Special Collections Administrative Offices University Librarian's Office Blind Students Study Room
FLOOR	Books. Class A-K
FLOOR	Card Catalog Circulation Department Reserve Books Interlibrary Loan Reference Department Public Services Office Periodical Information Office
FLOOR	Periodicals Current and Bound Newspapers Government Documents
FLOOR	Audiovisual Department Copying Services

Georgetown University, Washington, D.C.

person accept responsibility for keeping track of the changes that will be needed in the next edition.

Printing and Design

The printing and design of the handbook should be considered during the planning stage. If the library has a graphic design consultant, consult this person. Explore all possibilities and carefully evaluate the costs and advantages and disadvantages of each. Does the college or university have a printing service or instructional aids section from which advice can be obtained? Visit these offices and those of the local printers and designers to discuss your ideas, various options, and costs. The handbook can range in style from a typewritten sheet to a glossy, typeset, multicolored production. Note, however, that the cost does not necessarily reflect the effectiveness and attractiveness of the book.

Consider enlisting the help of student or faculty artists or photographers in designing the handbook's format, particularly the cover. The cover, which must catch the patron's eye in order to be effective, is the single most important design element, and the most expensive to produce. The old adage notwithstanding, people do judge books by their covers, and the handbook must first be noticed if it is to be used. Although it is not necessary to spend lots of money to produce an attractive handbook, the handbook nobody picks up, or the shoddy production which is glanced at briefly and then tossed away, benefits no one and is a waste of money, no matter how little it cost.

BIBLIOGRAPHIES, TOPICAL GUIDES, AND OTHER PRINTED GUIDES

Another method of instructing the library user through the printed word is by means of the bibliography or topical guide. The bibliography, for instructional purposes, is usually a straightforward listing of sources of information on a particular topic or for a particular discipline. It is most frequently handed out at library instruction sessions, to serve as a basis for discussion and for future reference by the student. Many libraries also compile bibliographies designed for certain disciplines: "Guide to Resources in Psychology" or "Selected Basic Reference Works in American Literature." These range from typewritten, duplicated sheets, to impressively printed little volumes. The most elaborate examples are the professionally published book catalogs of a library's holdings on a particular topic. The topical guide places more emphasis on search strategy than the traditional bibliography, and for this reason may be preferable for users who have not had the benefit of an instruction session. The bibliography, especially when compiled on a timely topic, may cause "recommended" books or articles to subsequently become so heavily used that they are unavailable to many would-be users. For this reason the topical guide is often a good format to adopt when faced with a large group of undergraduates all working on the same topics, whereas the standard bibliography, which allows more detail on specific sources, may be a wiser choice for graduate courses or small, specialized seminars.

Bibliographies

Let's first look at the traditional bibliography as it might be used in three different situations. We'll begin with course-related instruction. Let us say an introductory psychology class is coming for a one-hour library instruction session in preparation for working on library research papers. Most of the students are freshmen or sophomores. Many have never used the library. What type of bibliography will be appropriate? Should it start with the *Readers' Guide,* the *Social Sciences Index,* and lead up to *Psych Abstracts*? Or should it start with *Psych Abstracts* and move on to *Social Sciences Citation Index, Serials in Psychology,* and detailed specialized handbooks, dictionaries, and bibliographies? Should it be a ten-page bibliography that the students will be able to refer to when they go on to more advanced work, or should it be a two- or three-page handout accompanied by instructions to come to the desk for more help?

There is obviously no one way to approach the problem. Many libraries have a "basic bibliography" which includes some standard Wilson indexes, information on the card catalog arrangement, the Library of Congress Subject Headings, the location of periodicals and newspapers, and a few basic reference works. Such a list, which can be handed out to introductory classes and accompanied by a supplement geared to a particular course or assignment, can be a great time saver.

Although it is tempting to make each bibliography as individualized as possible, perhaps to the extent of listing appropriate sources for particular students' topics, it can involve much work to create a one-time-only bibliography. It is often wise to limit such details to an oral presentation.

It may help to number the items in a bibliography to be used in the classroom, for ease in referring to items and for flexibility in changing the order in which they are discussed. It is also possible to include lists of suggested subject terms for various indexes, and perhaps examples from the *Library of Congress Subject Headings* geared to the particular course or the students' assignments.

As a second example of use of the traditional bibliography, let's consider the bibliography designed for the graduate or advanced student in the field of psychology. This might be a definitive guide to "Basic Reference Materials in Psychology" in a particular library and would probably refer the user to other, more detailed sources of general information, such as White's *Guide to Information in the Social Sciences* and essential psychology reference materials. Such a bibliography might be used for advanced classes, and also be distributed to the psychology department or at a "How to do Research in Psychology" seminar. Copies could be kept on hand in the reference desk drawer or distributed through display racks. This bibliography could possibly be given to an introductory class, supplemented with a basic bibliography and words of caution. For the advanced user, the traditional bibliography suitable for many different topics within a wide discipline and applicable to many levels of research may be preferable to the briefer, more directive topical guide.

As a third example, let us take the type of bibliography that may be more common in public than in academic libraries. This is the list of materials on a topic of current interest. It may be distributed from standard display racks, from reference desks, or from an exhibit on the topic. It may also be sent to various academic departments. The purpose of such a bibliography is usually to draw attention to particular books, articles, or other media. Such a bibliography may be an extensive list of materials with little discussion of each or it may include fewer items with lengthy critical reviews. In either case, its purpose is to draw attention to the particular items mentioned, rather than to instruct in search strategy on a particular topic as a topical guide would do. For this type of bibliography in particular, a pleasing, consistent format may attract the patron and help readily identify the publication.

Topical Guides

Topical guides, especially those relating to specific popular subjects, can save staff time at reference desks and be a great aid to those students who hate to ask for help. They can also give a student more thorough answers to the question of how to find information on a certain topic than is sometimes possible to provide at a busy desk. The time saved in repeating certain basics over and over may later be spent helping that same student with a more difficult problem as he or she delves deeper into the topic. Commercial topical guides are available, but many libraries have designed their own.

"Library Pathfinders"[4] were developed at the Massachusetts Institute of Technology under a grant from the

Council on Library Resources. A similar product is the "LC Science Tracer Bullet"[5] developed by the Reference Section of the Science and Technology Division of the Library of Congress. But these commercial guides have drawbacks. Each library is unique. Every library will not have all of the resources listed, the individual library's locations and call numbers will be lacking, and new acquisitions will constantly need to be added. The best topical guides are usually those prepared to meet the needs of a particular library and its patrons.

Elements of Topical Guides

The object of a topical guide is to help a student begin a search for relevant material on a particular topic. It is not meant to be a complete and exhaustive bibliography. Most guides, whether commercial or homemade, include many or all of the following elements:

1. DEFINITION OR SCOPE — The topic should be defined and any jargon or specialized terms should be explained.

2. INTRODUCTION — One source, such as an encyclopedia article, that gives an overall discussion of the topic is valuable.

3. CARD CATALOG — Subject headings used in the card catalog to find books on the topic are indicated. Some guides will point out which terms are the best to use. The "Pathfinders"[6] have the subject headings labeled with terms such as "highly relevant," "relevant," and "general."

4. BOOKS — If books are included in the guide, this will probably be its weakest part. Choosing four or five "good," "classic," or "available" books does not mean that

these are the best books on the subject. The publication of new books will cause the guide to become dated unless some of them are added.

5. REFERENCE BOOKS	Special handbooks or encyclopedias are often listed in this section.
6. BIBLIOGRAPHIES	This can sometimes be the most valuable section of a topical guide. Bibliographies can be selected from the card catalog, *Bibliography Index,* or periodical articles.
7. PERIODICAL INDEXES	Periodical indexes that contain relevant material should be listed. They will lead the students beyond *Readers' Guide* to professional and scholarly material. Some guides list the proper subject headings to use in each index, a feature which adds to the usefulness of the guide.
8. PROCEEDINGS, REPORTS, DOCUMENTS	Depending on the topic, there may be relevant materials in these categories which deserve individual treatment.

Not every topical guide must include all of the above elements. The holdings of a particular library, the needs of the students, and the time available to develop guides should all be taken into consideration.

Promoting the Guides

Make the guides eye catching. Colorful paper or artistic designs will help attract students. Make the guides accessible. This may be accomplished through the use of guide cards in the card catalog and/or attractive display of the guides. Keep them simple to use. This does not mean that difficult bibliographic tools should not be included, but the format should be obvious to anyone using the guide. Keep

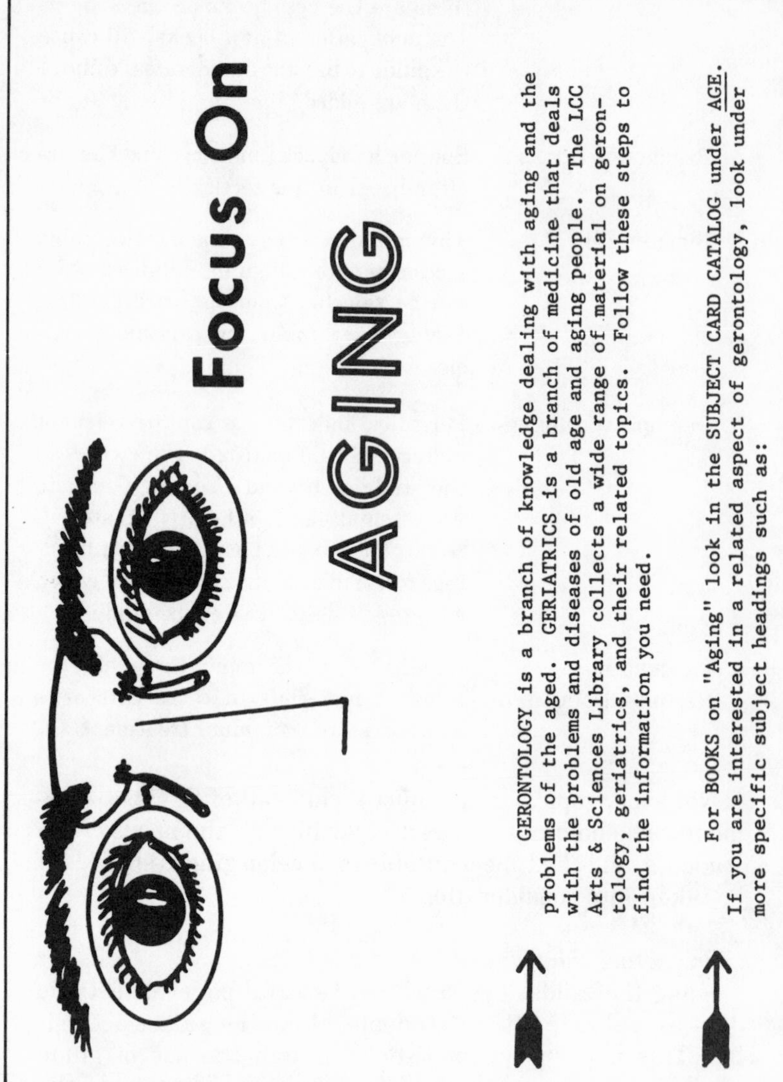

Focus On AGING

GERONTOLOGY is a branch of knowledge dealing with aging and the problems of the aged. GERIATRICS is a branch of medicine that deals with the problems and diseases of old age and aging people. The LCC Arts & Sciences Library collects a wide range of material on gerontology, geriatrics, and their related topics. Follow these steps to find the information you need.

For BOOKS on "Aging" look in the SUBJECT CARD CATALOG under AGE. If you are interested in a related aspect of gerontology, look under more specific subject headings such as:

Reprinted with permission from Lansing Community College,

AGED	GERIATRICS	OLD AGE
AGING	MIDDLE AGE	OLD AGE ASSISTANCE
AGE AND EMPLOYMENT	NURSING HOMES	OLD AGE HOMES
		RETIREMENT

A complete list of subject headings used in the card catalog related to the topic of aging may be found in the Library of Congress Subject Headings (two large red volumes located near the card catalog).

It is not possible to go directly to the shelves and browse through the books related to aging. Due to the library's re-classification project, books on the subject are in two classification systems. Books that have been re-classified, or are new, have Library of Congress (LC) call numbers beginning with a letter combination such as HV 1451. Books purchased before 1976, and not yet re-classified, have Dewey Decimal (DDC) call numbers beginning with 301, 362, or 613 depending upon the subject of the book.

The best approach is to check the specific subjects in the card catalog, write down the call numbers of the books that appeal to you and then browse in the area where those books are found.

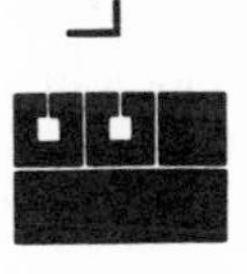

Lansing Community College
Dept. of Library Services

Department of Library Services.

them up-to-date. Periodically revise subject headings and terminology. New editions of reference books or texts should be noted. Clearly indicate the location of the reference tools listed in the guide. This will avoid numerous directional questions. Keep a current list of the guides. Copies of such a list could be posted near a display. Distribution to faculty may help with public relations. Make the guides accurate. Misleading information can easily destroy the credibility of the guides. Suggest that students use the guides when the occasion arises. Students may have passed by the display or not come across the guide cards in the card catalog.

Other Printed Guides

In addition to traditional bibliographies and pathfinders or topical guides, there is a third category of miscellaneous printed guides. Sometimes these combine elements of the topical guide in suggesting subject headings for particular types of information, and those of the library skills workbook in providing instruction on the use of particular tools. The University of Texas at Austin, for example, has an excellent series of "Study Guides," ranging from the general "Using the Library for Research" to more specific guides, to which the student is referred in the general ones, which include "Using Encyclopedias for Research," "Finding Information in Periodicals," and "Finding Book Reviews."

Some libraries have prepared their own "point-of-use" guides to specific reference works. The Milton S. Eisenhower Library at Johns Hopkins, for example, has a series of guides which include such items as "Guide to the ERIC *Current Index to Journals in Education,*" complete with flow charts and sample citations.

Other libraries have devised printed guides to "Job Finding Aids" (Johns Hopkins) or "Bibliographic Citations" (Johns Hopkins), and "How to Write a Term Paper: Search Strategy" (Penn State). Students occasionally request information on how to write book reviews, business letters, or structure an argument—topics for which it is often difficult to come up with ready reference answers at a moment's notice. Guides to some sources for this type of information are helpful to both staff and students.

Lansing Community College has an eye-catching series entitled "Focus on . . ." printed with an arresting pair of eyes at the top of a single sheet printed in colored ink on colored paper. The guide to film reviews, for example, lists appropriate card catalog subject headings, appropriate call numbers for browsing in both the LC and Dewey systems, a listing of collections of film reviews, and appropriate subject headings in such standard sources as *Readers' Guide, New York Times Index,* and *Newsbank—Review of the Arts.*

The University of Michigan publishes an attractive twelve-page booklet entitled "How to Use the Card Catalog of the Collections in the Libraries of the University of Michigan." This publication is obviously not aimed at the casual user who dashes in to look something up quickly, but for the serious student or researcher it presents essential information about the catalog that would be difficult to convey in any other way.

DEVISING AN OVERALL PLAN

It isn't necessary that a library have every possible type of printed guide. Some libraries rely on a handbook and a very few signs. Others—the University of Kentucky, for example—have many graphic aids in the building and extensive collections of printed guides: a conventional handbook, information sheets, subject bibliographies, a library guides series, a library seminar series of bibliographies, and a series of subject guides to research, not to mention various library-skills workbooks. The first task in launching a series of printed guides is to look carefully at the library's needs and consult with other members of the public-service staff, faculty, and students. As with the handbook, the types of questions most commonly asked at the service desks can be the best indication of what is needed.

An overwhelming number of students writing papers on abortion, battered wives, child abuse, Southeast Asia, or al-

THE UNIVERSITY OF KENTUCKY LIBRARY GUIDES

HOW TO FIND A PERIODICAL ARTICLE

Journal articles are important to research since they often provide the latest information on a topic. While the card catalog lists journal titles, it does not include information on individual articles. To find articles on a given topic, you need to consult a periodical index. To determine which index is relevant to your topic, refer to the library guide on indexes.

Most indexes are issued annually and have an author/subject arrangement. If you encounter any difficulty in locating a specific topic in an index, **ask for assistance at the Reference Desk.** Once you have found the article you want, copy the complete citation—author and title of article, journal title, volume, date and pages. In a citation, the journal title often appears in abbreviated form and a key at the front of the volume gives the full title for each abbreviation. Be sure to write down the full title as this is what is needed to find the journal in the card catalog.

Reprinted with permission of Instructional Services,

To locate a periodical in the University of Kentucky library system, check the title of the journal in the author/title card catalog. Remember that if the name of the issuing agency appears in the title, the journal will usually be entered under the name of that agency. For example, to find the *Journal of Home Economics*, look under *Journal*, but to find the *Journal of the American Medical Association*, look under *American.*

If you do not find a particular title in the catalog, ask for assistance at the Reference Desk. Often on a periodical card there is a note "For Holdings see Periodical File" or "Holdings Listed in Central Serial Records." This has nothing to do with the location of the actual volumes but only tells the user that the receipt of each issue of that journal was recorded on a card in Central Serial Records.

Most periodicals issued by the federal government, state government and the United Nations are not listed in the card catalog. For information concerning these items, check with the Government Publications Department.

As a rule, journals do not circulate. If you wish a copy of a particular article, there are copying machines available on the first and second floors of the library.

University of Kentucky.

The University of Michigan
Undergraduate Library

GUIDE TO PREPARING RESEARCH PAPERS

The research paper presents the results of careful investigation of a subject. To be successful, it must clearly express facts and ideas and it must accurately document sources used. Preparation is the key to writing a good research paper; preparation includes finding information, selecting and interpreting data, and evaluating source materials. This guide is intended to help you produce a successful research paper by suggesting a research strategy which will enable you to fully exploit the UGLi's resources.

I. Choose a topic

A. Select a general topic which interests you and which falls within the scope of your assignment.

B. Obtain background information.
1. Familiarize yourself with facts, trends, concepts, and terminology by consulting
a. A general encyclopedia such as the Encyclopedia Americana or the Encyclopaedia Britannica for an introduction to your subject.
b. A subject encyclopedia such as the Encyclopedia of Education or the Encyclopedia of World Art for specialized information.
c. An article or chapter in a textbook, a history, or a survey for an overview of your topic.
2. Look at the bibliographies which may accompany these background sources to identify likely sources of further information.

C. Limit your topic.
1. Briefly outline the facts and concepts which you already know.
2. Write out questions which can be asked about your topic.

Reprinted with permission of the University of Michigan Libraries.

coholism may suggest topical guides on these topics. Or take a cue from current international, national, and local news, in hopes of anticipating students' needs while simultaneously encouraging them to become better informed about important issues. The strengths and weaknesses of the library's collection might be a starting point if the collection contains a wealth of resources of particular topics which might be used if only the students knew they were there. The students may be weary of some of the ever- and over-popular topics, but unable to think of anything new. Compiling and displaying bibliographies or topical guides may help.

On the other hand, the variety of topics on which students seek assistance may be too great to make topical guides feasible, but there are constant requests for ways to locate speeches, film reviews, plays in collections, or editorials. This type of guide may require less frequent revision than the timely-subject guide. If there are many requests for explanations of the card catalog, certain periodical indexes, or the arrangement of periodicals and newspapers, a series of guides to these may be the place to start. Another approach is to work with instructors on class assignments. Instead of course-related instruction sessions, it may be possible in some instances to design search strategy outlines for specific assignments for those courses.

In deciding which approach or approaches to take with printed guides, consider how they fit into the total instructional program. A well-coordinated series in consistent format will be more effective than random issues. As with the handbook, matters such as design, ease of revision, and distribution should be thought out before beginning. Is the publication to be distributed for one specific course-related session or to a whole series of sessions? Is it to be kept at the reference desk to be given out only upon request? Will copies be distributed to the faculty in certain departments? Will a display be set up for self-service? Is it to be "point-of-use"? The answers to these questions should be taken into consideration when work is begun on the publication.

SIGNS

The role of signs in libraries is receiving increased attention. While earlier books on library planning and design

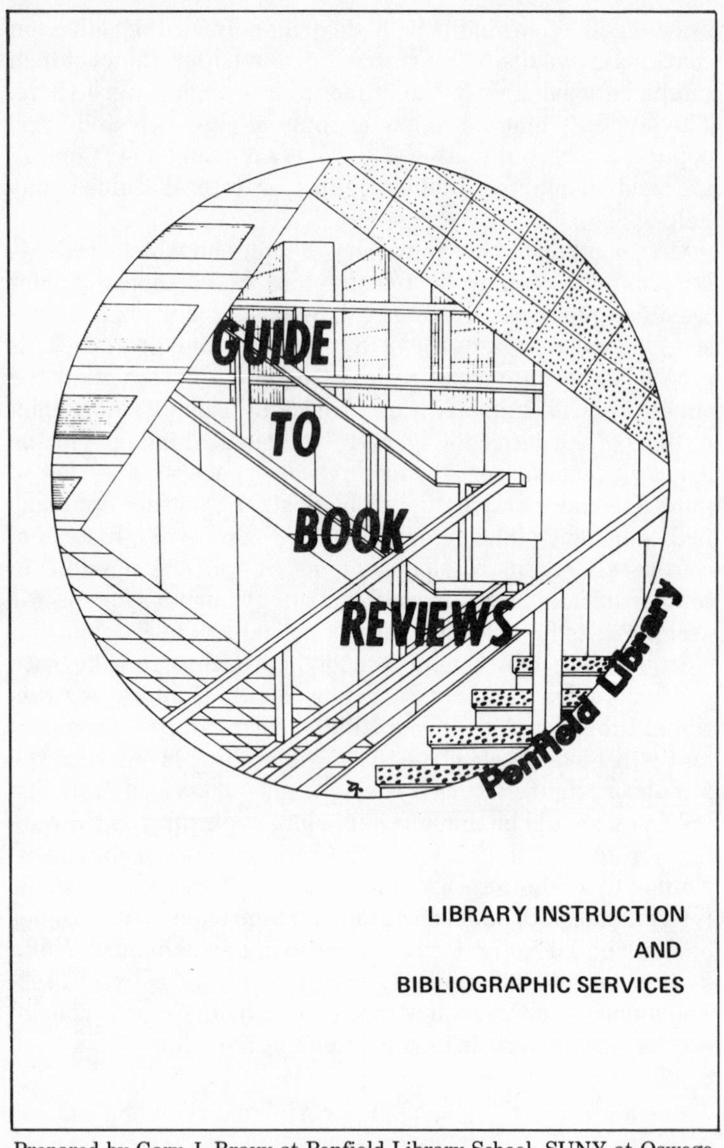

Prepared by Gary J. Bravy at Penfield Library School, SUNY at Oswego.

BOOK REVIEWS are often a convenient method of locating evaluative information about a book. In order to use the following book review guides, you will need to know: (1) the author's name; (2) the title of the book; (3) the year the book was published. Publication date can usually be found on the title page or its reverse (or on the book's card in our catalog), and is particularly important as most of the book review guides are cumulated yearly. Be sure to check both the year of publication and the previous and following year as reviews are often published well before or after a book's "official" publication date. Do not hesitate to ask for help at the reference desk if you need assistance. **ALL** of the following are located in the lobby near the Abstract Room.

BOOK REVIEW DIGEST. 1905–

Indexes and excerpts reviews from American and British journals. Short summary of the book precedes the review citations and excerpts. Arranged alphabetically by author of the book, or title when applicable. Published monthly, cumulated yearly. Cumulated yearly and quinquennial indexes with title and subject listing (no cumulated author index). Indexes a wide range of books, both fiction and non-fiction. Highly specialized or technical books generally not included. Children's books included. A major source and perhaps the first place to check for reviews of fiction and general non-fiction.

BOOK REVIEW INDEX. 1965–

Alphabetical citations by author of book reviewed. Indexes reviews in over 200 magazines and journals, mainly in the humanities and social sciences. Well over 50,000 reviews are included in each annual cumulation. Books not found in *Book Review Digest* may often be found here. Indexes books that have received few or even a single review in journals covered. Includes fiction, non-fiction, and children's books. Published bi-monthly, cumulated annually.

LIBRARY JOURNAL BOOK REVIEW. 1967–

Full reprints of reviews from *Library Journal.* Author and title index; reviews are arranged in a subject order. Broad coverage of both fiction and non-fiction. Reviews are generally short, concise, and comparative in nature.

seldom mentioned sign systems, Langmead and Beckman's *New Library Design*[7] includes some helpful sections on the matter. The most useful and comprehensive book to date is Spencer and Reynolds' *Directional Signing and Labelling in Libraries and Museums: A Review of Current Theory and Practice.*[8] Especially helpful are the summaries of research in the field, recommendations for areas of further research, and examples of good and bad sign practices. A new book which promises to be helpful is Dorothy Pollet and Peter C. Haskell's *Sign Systems for Libraries: Solving the Wayfinding Problem.*[9]

Most discussions of signs in libraries distinguish between functions of signs. Langmead and Beckman divide them into labeling, functional, and instructional.[10] Labeling signs are those that number and/or label rooms, exits, and so on. Functional signs include such information as "present briefcases for checking," and "elevators for staff use only." Instructional signs include such information as how to use the card catalog, how to use the serials list, and how to find a book.

The total sign system of the library should be taken into account in planning instructional signs. Spencer and Reynolds note: "The standard of directional signing and guiding in most of the libraries visited was poor."[11] There appeared to be little coordination of the visual appearance of "signs, notices, instructions, labels, stationery and printed information."[12] The result was an overall effect of "sloppiness and disorganization."[13]

Most writers on library signing recommend the hiring of a design consultant. This may seem to be very expensive, but in the long run is cost effective. Spencer and Reynolds argue that a coordinated system of graphics will make a favorable impression on visitors and even help create a friendlier attitude toward the library.[14] It will also raise staff morale by alleviating the irritation resulting from repeatedly responding to the same directional questions over and over again. Spencer and Reynolds feel good signage save time for both staff and visitors, and suggest that even vandalism and grafitti may be reduced.

There tends to be a feeling among librarians that no one pays any attention to signs, and therefore they're not worth having. If the signs are unsightly, cluttered, confused, and uncoordinated, this may very well be true. Yet even then, there is probably a certain percentage of people who would rather struggle through on their own than ask for help. Spencer and Reynolds cite a study which showed that 21 percent of the undergraduates using a university library were reluctant to ask for help.[15]

Designing effective instructional signs is difficult, and ineffective signs may be scarcely better than none at all. Yet signs can be an important part of a total instructional program. They should be well coordinated with various other forms of printed instructions and active instruction, as well as with a total library sign system.

SUMMARY

Printed guides to libraries, whether in the form of booklets, simple handouts, or signs, provide an essential service. Well-designed guides save patrons from some of the frustration arising from having to either search blindly or ask trivial questions. They also enable the library staff to provide better service to those who do ask for help. Such guides are invaluable instructional aids, whether used in classroom presentations, for independent study, or as a substitute for oral presentations. They frequently present information more clearly and concisely than oral communication (one picture is worth a thousand words) and provide the patron with a record to be referred to as needed.

Libraries may well look to department stores, airports, world fairs, Disneyland, and museums for ideas for printed guides and sign systems that will make libraries more pleasant and more useful, both to the first-time user and the returning patron. As personnel costs rise, printed guides may become increasingly important in all library public-service and instructional programs.

FOOTNOTES

1. Malcolm B. Stevenson, "Progress in Documentation: Education of Users of Libraries and Information Services," *Journal of Documentation,* 33: 64 (March 1977).
2. U.S. Federal Library Committee, *Guidelines for Library Handbooks* (Bethesda, Md.: ERIC Educational Document Reproduction Service, ED 067 137, 1972).
3. Ibid., p. 4.
4. Charles H. Stevens, Marie P. Canfield, and Jeffrey J. Gardner, "Library Pathfinders: A New Possibility for Cooperative Reference Service," *College and University Libraries,* 34: 40-46 (January 1973).
5. *LC Science Tracer Bullet,* Science and Technology Division (Washington, D.C.: Library of Congress).
6. Stevens et al., pp. 40-46.
7. Stephen Langmead and Margaret Beckman, *New Library Design: Guidelines to Planning Academic Library Buildings* (Toronto: Wiley, 1970).
8. Herbert Spencer and Linda Reynolds, *Directional Signing and Labelling in Libraries and Museums: A Review of Current Practice* (London: Royal College of Art, 1977).
9. Dorothy Pollet and Peter C. Haskell, *Sign Systems for Libraries: Solving the Wayfinding Problem* (New York: Bowker, 1979).
10. Langmead and Beckman, p. 66.
11. Spencer and Reynolds, p. 6.
12. Ibid.
13. Ibid.
14. Ibid., p. 8.
15. Ibid., p. 63.

SUGGESTED READINGS

Library Handbooks

Fox, Peter. "Library Handbooks: An International Viewpoint." *Libri* 27 (December 1977): 296-304.

Griffith, Alice B. "Library Handbook Standards." *Wilson Library Bulletin* 39 (February 1965): 475-7.

Kazemak, Francis E. "Library Handbooks and Orientation in Illinois Community College Libraries." *Illinois Libraries* 57 (May 1975): 354-5.

McCormick, Mona. "Library Handbooks and Other Printed Bibliographic Aids," in John Lubans, Jr., ed., *Educating the Library User,* pp. 307-317. New York: Bowker, 1974.

Miller, Mary Celine. "Library Handbooks, College and University," in *Encyclopedia of Library and Information Science,* Vol. 15, pp. 282-294. New York: Dekker, 1968- .

U.S. Federal Library Committee. *Guidelines for Library Handbooks.* Bethesda. ERIC Document Reproduction Service 1972. ED 067 137.

Signs

Carey, R. J. P. *Library Guiding: A Program for Exploiting Library Resources.* London: Bingley, 1973.

Crosby/Fletcher/Forbes. *A Sign Systems Manual.* New York: Praeger, 1970.

Langmead, Stephen, and Beckman, Margaret. *New Library Design: Guidelines to Planning Academic Library Buildings.* Toronto: Wiley, 1970.

Pollet, Dorothy. "You Can Get There from Here: New Directions in Library Signage." *Wilson Library Bulletin* 50 (February 1976): 456-62.

Pollet, Dorothy and Haskell, Peter C. *Sign Systems for Libraries: Solving the Wayfinding Problem.* New York: Bowker, 1979.

Spencer, Herbert and Reynolds, Linda. *Directional Signing and Labelling in Libraries and Museums: A Review of Current Theory and Practice.* London: Readability of Print Research Unit, Royal College of Art, 1977. (Available from the publisher, 6A Cromwell Place, London, SW7 2NJ. $14.)

CHAPTER 4

Course-Related Instruction

INTRODUCTION

Course-related instruction, an outgrowth of the library instruction movement of the sixties and seventies, appears to be today's most popular mode of library instruction. It is usually defined as instruction in the library skills and bibliographic information necessary to complete the objectives of a particular nonlibrary course. A library session is scheduled in cooperation with a course instructor, and is usually offered during one session of class time.

A related term, course-integrated instruction, is used somewhat less frequently, and implies a closer relationship between the objectives of the course and its library component. In such a case the librarian may be involved with the instructor from the very beginning in planning the objectives of the course and its library component. The two terms reflect differing degrees of involvement of the library with the course. Many librarians constantly endeavor to bring their course-related sessions closer to the ideal of course-integrated ones. Because a sharp distinction between the terms is difficult to maintain, the phrase course-related will be used to cover both ends of the spectrum, unless a certain example is unquestionably course-integrated.

ADVANTAGES

There are many reasons for the current popularity of course-related instruction. For one, it is a type of activity which readily lends itself to the kind of grassroots efforts with which it has been associated. It is the kind of activity which an individual librarian, perceiving a need, can take on as an extension of the one-to-one instruction that occurs at the reference desk. It may often begin like this: the librarian finds that there have been several requests for a particular type of information within a very short time period. After questioning one of the students about the nature of the course and the assignment, a telephone call is made to the instructor of the class. This call will alert the instructor that a number of students have been asking for help with their assignments. At the same time, it could also be suggested that the instructor might like to have a librarian talk to the class to get the students started on their projects, give them a brief explanation of some of the essential reference works in the field, and discuss some techniques for locating information on their topics. The instructor may respond to this proposal with disinterest, caution, or enthusiasm. With a little practice the librarian learns the best approaches to take with faculty members. If this instructor cannot spare the time this term, how about next term? In this manner the foundation for many course-related instruction programs have been laid.

Although the benefits of planning comprehensive instructional programs have been emphasized elsewhere in this book, course-related instruction has the advantage of allowing one to start small, carefully feeling one's way, assessing needs and success, and eventually develop a program uniquely suited to the needs of a particular institution. If the program succeeds and grows, detailed planning and coordination will undoubtedly be needed; yet if the program falls short of expectations and another approach is decided upon, little or nothing is lost.

A few small successes may even change the opinions of

unsupportive administrators, colleagues, and faculty members. If initial attempts at course-related instruction are successful, chances are that there will soon be more requests than can easily be handled. This is the time to look at the total program, do some serious planning, and request support.

A second advantage of the course-related approach is that it is an excellent means of building good library-faculty relations. Discussions between librarians and faculty about what each is trying to do can be beneficial to both. The roles should be complementary; yet all too often, in traditional situations, there is little contact between the two. Librarians are preoccupied with library matters, faculty members are concerned with lectures, assignments, and research, and the student, who should be the primary concern of both, may be lost in the shuffle. Librarians view the student from one perspective; professors, from another. By sharing perspectives, each could be more effective. Course-related instruction provides an area for both to meet and acquire understanding and respect for each other.

A third benefit of course-related instruction is its potential impact on the curriculum. When librarians and instructors work together—and here we are entering the domain of course-integrated instruction—the nature of the courses themselves may change, with more emphasis placed on independent library investigation as an integral part of the course.

Such a change may also have considerable impact on the use of library materials, placing heavier demands on both the collection and the staff. It is at this point that a panic-stricken cry of protest often arises from librarians and administrators opposed to instruction: "We can't afford it! We don't have the staff!" Although difficulties can arise from a great increase in demand for materials and services, and changes in routines may have to be made, such a result should be considered a success, and be used to justify increased expenditures for materials and services.

A fourth advantage of course-related instruction is its flexibility. Unlike a credit course, which must be planned far in advance and follow a prescribed syllabus, the course-related session does not require such extensive investment of a librarian's time. The session can be scheduled well in advance or on brief notice if a need arises and the library is able to comply. The content of the session can be varied to fit the demands of the course, and free experimentation made of various techniques. The session can be held within the library or in the regular classroom, depending on such factors as available classroom space in the library, the size of the class, and the necessity for demonstrating certain library materials or equipment.

A fifth advantage of course-related instruction is its ability to reach a fairly large number of students. Since each class normally devotes only one class period to a library lecture, it may be possible for one librarian to meet with five or more classes per term. If there is an average of 30 students per class, one librarian has the potential of contacting 150 or more students. If there are four librarians involved in instruction, and they each teach five classes of 30 students each, 500 students may benefit from the library sessions offered. Included within these classes are those students who, for a variety of reasons, may never ask for individual help at a service desk.

The personal contact of the student with the librarian as teacher is a sixth advantage of course-related instruction. It tends to make the librarian more approachable. Often students will come to a reference desk and ask specifically for the librarian who taught their session, even though their questions could be answered by anyone at the desk.

Students often are amazed that there is so much to know about library materials and how they are organized. Prior to library instruction sessions, they may not have believed that the person who sits at the reference desk could possibly know much that would be of value to them. The personal contact with the librarian in the classroom frequently changes this perception, and they realize that there is, in fact, so much to learn that they need not be afraid of appearing stupid if they ask for help.

A final advantage of course-related instruction—and this is the one most frequently cited—is its ability to meet student needs at the appropriate time. The session can be scheduled to coincide with students' selection of term paper topics, when their need to know "how to find out" is most pressing. The session can not only address this need at the appropriate time; it can also focus on the specific interests of the students, especially if a list of chosen topics is available to the librarian ahead of time. When students are required to make immediate use of what they have learned in the course-related session, the learning is reinforced and is thus longer lasting. An additional advantage for the librarian is that these attentive, interested, highly-motivated students are a joy to teach.

DISADVANTAGES

With so many advantages, what prevents course-related instruction from universal acceptance as the preferred means of library instruction? One of the major problems is its high cost in terms of time and personnel. Even if one librarian can reach many more students through course-related than through credit instruction, there are still not enough librarians with enough time to reach all the students in a large university. In addition, many librarians lack training and experience in teaching and are therefore reluctant to teach. This places an additional burden on the few who are involved. It is for these reasons that, although course-related instruction may often be considered ideal, there is such a proliferation of workbook programs, programmed texts, printed guides, and other means of indirect instruction.

There are also other problems. One arises from the need to respond to existing class schedules. By attempting to meet every class at a time coinciding with the assignment of paper topics, most instruction is crowded into the early and middle parts of a term. For three to four weeks librarians are teaching continuously, and classrooms and equipment are scheduled to the hilt. Then comes the lull. With careful planning, courses can be scheduled and assigned in advance, and the lull used for preparation and evaluation; nevertheless, this concentration of instruction into a few weeks of the term further restricts the number of sessions a limited number of librarians can teach.

A second problem, from the teaching librarian's point of view, is the risk of continual repetition of the same one-hour routine presentation term after term, sometimes several times a term. Also related to the short time span is the difficulty of achieving satisfactory follow-up and evaluation in a single session. Unlike the regular course instructor, who can design assignments which test the students' progress, and can work with students on a daily basis throughout the term and assist them in their progress, the librarian of the course-related session will probably see the students only once, or at the most two or three times, if they come back to the library specifically requesting help from him or her. As a result the librarian teaching a number of course-related sessions often becomes frustrated at constantly giving and never seeing evidence of results.

Although there are ways of getting feedback during the presentation, and evaluation forms can be sent to the students and the instructor following the session, and although the librarian can arrange to assist the instructor in evaluating the library-research aspect of the students' papers, all of these methods require extra work for both the librarian and the instructor and are therefore often ignored. Even if they are used, these methods are not always satisfying.

The time limitations of the single session also place severe constraints on how much the students can absorb. A one-hour session can be overwhelming for the neophyte library user. In addition, in any given class one usually encounters students with widely varying experience in the use of the library. In almost any course-related session there will be some who are bewildered by the complexity of the information presented and others who will find it repetitious. It is difficult to meet the needs of everyone.

ORGANIZING FOR COURSE-RELATED INSTRUCTION

The first question to be decided in implementing a course-related instruction program is who the library teaching staff will be. There are widely differing philosophies on this issue, and the differences become visible when we look at individual programs. There is one group which strongly believes that libraries and the teaching of library skills are solely the domain of the librarian. In some libraries, only certain librarians are designated to teach. Often these individuals are subject or instructional specialists. At the other end of the scale, there are librarians who teach faculty members rather than students. The faculty, in turn, teaches library skills to its classes.

In looking at various programs of course-related instruction, four distinct staffing patterns emerge:

1. designated instructional librarians within the library;
2. broad involvement by most or all librarians;
3. the instructional coordinator with the involvement of interested librarians from both public and technical services;
4. outside instructors (regular faculty, teaching assistants, etc.).

In the first pattern, it is understood that the instructional librarian(s) will do all of the classroom instruction. This situation exists in many academic libraries, frequently as the result of the enthusiasm of a few and the reluctance of others to become involved with instruction. There are definite advantages to this pattern of organization. Such designated librarians are strongly committed to library instruction. Many enjoy being in the classroom and teaching, and this is obvious in their presentations and attitudes. Since instruction is their primary job, there is time allotted them for classroom presentations, faculty contacts, and the preparation of handouts and support material. The instructional librarian is often able to work closely with the faculty. The task of planning class assignments which involve the library is shared by the librarian and faculty member. This working relationship also offers opportunities for the librarian to evaluate students' papers, literature searches, and bibliographies.

There are some disadvantages to this approach. The first is what can be termed as the "burnt-out syndrome." Teaching the same material over and over again becomes tedious and enervating. Most classes, no matter the level, need to review the basics: card catalog, periodical indexes, and serial listings. There are only so many exciting, innovative means of presenting these topics. An instructional librarian may cover the same material four times per week, thirty weeks of the year. After a period of time, it becomes difficult to remain enthusiastic, and this may become evident to the students. A second disadvantage is the limited staff available to teach. One or two individuals cannot cover all the potential classes. Programs must be limited to the availability of the instructional librarians. It should also be noted that instructional librarians can quickly lose touch with the needs of the students if they are not interacting with them at the service desks.

The second pattern of organizing for course-related instruction is to involve all the librarians. One model for this type of organization is at Sangamon State.

> Non-professionals perform original cataloging, acquisitions work, circulation services, media production and distribution, interlibrary loan and government documents processing. What are the professionals doing? They are teaching faculty and students how to use the library.[1]

This approach has worked at Sangamon State, and faculty, students, and librarians are reaping the benefits. The broad involvement of librarians has the advantage of sharing the role of instruction. The "burnt-out syndrome" can be avoided. Librarians are teaching classes that fall in their subject or interest areas. The library has focused on library instruction and everyone is part of the team effort.

Although this approach may seem best, there are pitfalls. Realistically, not all librarians are suited for teaching. Forcing such individuals into a teaching situation can be a mistake. Students are quick to spot weakness and inability. There may be a gradual replacement of nonteaching librarians, but this will be due to attrition and retirements over the years.

Since many libraries are well established, it would take a complete administrative restructuring to adapt the Sangamon State model. Acceptance of instruction as a primary activity is essential. Instruction does take time, and unless this is taken into consideration, librarians will be reluctant to take on an "overload" assignment. This seems to be particularly true with technical-operations librarians. In many libraries, instruction is over and above their daily activities.

The third pattern for staffing a course-related program is a simplified version of the Sangamon State model. A core of interested public and technical-services staff can be successfully utilized, particularly if there is strong leadership. The instructional coordinator must assume an important role in this pattern. It is this person who must be able to teach others to teach. By providing a program structure and the opportunity to train, others can quickly become confident and effective teachers. Eventually, the initial group of instructors can grow and expand as new members become involved. The advantages to this approach include a greater flexibility for scheduling classes and a healthy involvement of the various departments throughout the library. The coordinator is also able to build and maintain an acceptable level of teaching competency for the classes being taught.

The greatest disadvantage to this approach is the fact that involvement in the program is almost totally dependent on the good will and interest of those volunteering. In some libraries it becomes an uphill battle to try to attract the busy staff to add one more activity to their schedules. Also, if key individuals retire or resign, the program must find someway to take up the slack. The coordinator is in the awkward situation of continually asking for volunteers, and this approach hardly guarantees continuity for any program.

A fourth organizational pattern utilizes outside instructors. In recent years, many librarians have come to realize the importance of reaching the faculty. By teaching the faculty how to present library skills to their classes, the librarian reaches not only the class, but also the faculty member. There is also the advantage of reaching more students with minimal librarian involvement. The University of Maryland's undergraduate library tries to teach each class only once. After that, the instruction is turned over to the faculty. Librarians meet with the faculty each term and also provide bibliographies and handouts. Classroom space is reserved in the library.[2] Another library using the same approach with basic English classes is the University of Texas at Austin. A limited number of librarians reach a large number of faculty who, in turn, reach a large number of students.

The greatest weakness in this type of teaching pattern is the lack of quality control. Even though the librarian and faculty member work closely together, there is no guarantee that the information presented about the library is accurate. In addition, outside instructors do not have the librarian's depth of knowledge about the library.

There are individuals who claim their particular method is the best as well as the only way. There is no doubt that the strengths of each staffing pattern can be argued and the disadvantages minimized. But there is no right or wrong way. The pattern chosen should reflect the overall philosophy of the instructional program of each library.

IDENTIFYING TARGET COURSES

Once the staffing pattern has been determined, it must be decided which courses should be involved in the course-related instruction program. The most haphazard, and probably most common, method of identifying potential classes is by keeping track of the questions asked at the service desks. A poorly designed or difficult library assignment will often be evident in these questions. When the third or fourth student appears with the same type of question or when one student appears who is quite confused about an assignment, a library instruction session may be in order. Ask the students what class they are from and who their instructor is. Although it is normally too late to hold a class that term, it may be possible to anticipate the assignment the next time. Many faculty members are surprised to hear that their class is having problems with the assignment, and are often glad to be made aware of it.

A more organized approach to making contacts is by the use of publicity. Announcements at departmental faculty meetings or flyers in appropriate mail boxes will often alert faculty to the service offered. Personal phone calls are quite effective. One enterprising librarian managed to arrange a library class during a cocktail party.

There is a more organized method, however, of planning a comprehensive course-related program. Courses at most universities and colleges can be divided into three categories: lower-division undergraduate, upper-division undergraduate, and graduate. Most lower-division undergraduate courses are foundation courses. Students are attempting to master the basics of a subject field such as biology, mathematics, or psychology. Many of these courses emphasize factual information and essential concepts rather than research papers. Such "foundation" courses are usually not suitable for course-related instruction. Within the same lower-division group, however, there are some courses that are suitable for introducing library skills. Speech communication is a good example of one of these foundation courses. Since students are often assigned to find suitable material to support a speech they must make in their class, they can benefit from a session on the basic library materials available to them. Another target group might be the English composition classes, where short research papers are frequently required. Course descriptions listed in the college catalog are extremely helpful in determining course requirements. Any class that requires a paper can be a candidate for course-related sessions. To those looking at the possibility of teaching at the beginning level, a word of caution is in order. Careful consideration must be given to the enrollment figures. Frequently freshmen classes have high enrollments, and most libraries do not have the staff to teach multitudes of students.

Those in the second group, upper-level undergraduate courses, are often good candidates for course-related instruction. The classes tend to be smaller and the subject matter is more narrowly defined. Assignments often include research or term papers which require students to use the library. Frequently there is one course in each discipline that all majors must take. If such key courses can be identified, it is possible to provide library instruction for all students in those subject areas.

The final group is comprised of graduate courses. Most graduate programs include a mandatory research course. This course is often preliminary to thesis work. These are usually the most appropriate classes to bring into the library for course-related sessions. Motivation is usually not a problem at this level. Most graduate students are grateful for help.

Course-related sessions can work at all levels. Thoughtful planning can add structure and continuity to the overall program. Eventually a healthy instructional program will emerge that will serve the needs of the students.

ADMINISTRATIVE DETAILS

In addition to staffing and identifying targets for the course-related instruction program, there are many practical administrative details to be considered. First, there must be a point of contact. This could be the instructional coordinator's office, the reference desk, or a general public-service office. The telephone number and the name of a contact person should be included in all types of publicity as well as in the telephone book.

The office or area receiving the calls for instruction should have a written statement that includes guidelines under which classes will be accepted. What is the required amount of lead time? Two weeks? One week? Three days? Will high school and elementary groups be routinely scheduled? Must the class have a preassigned library project? Is the instructor required to be present for the class? A policy statement that includes responses to these questions is helpful in heading off awkward or questionable requests for library instruction classes.

In addition to a policy statement, it is beneficial to have a procedure manual. There are many details involved in a course-related program, and having them written down prevents panic when a key individual is ill or away from the library. The following items could be included:

1. directions for assigning individual librarians to specific classes
    a) what method is used to contact teaching librarian
    b) what supervisors and administrators must be informed
2. method for reserving AV equipment and any available classrooms
3. copies of form letters used to contact faculty and students
4. significant dates for publicity, flyers, phone contacts, etc.
5. directions for emergency or unusual situations (for example: the classroom door key is lost; librarian is ill)
6. the methods being used to keep statistics

Both the policy statement and procedures manual should be discussed with the entire library staff, and not arbitrarily issued. The document statements should be realistic. For example, it might be beneficial for the library to demand four weeks' notice for a class, but it is an unrealistic expectation. Once the policies are agreed upon and established, there should be adherence to these provisions. If one person accepts a fifth-grade class, it sets a precedent for this service to be demanded by others. Finally, all such documents should be updated regularly. An obsolete procedure manual or policy statement can do more harm than good.

METHODS OF PRESENTATION

Because presentation time is so limited in course-related sessions, its careful planning is essential. Every minute should count. This does not mean, however, that there should be sixty or ninety minutes of nonstop lecture. One of the primary goals in a course-related library session is to present relevant material while maintaining a high level of interest. The class session can include a variety of meaningful activities. Besides the lecture, it may be beneficial to use a slide-tape program. Transparencies are a good change of pace. Classroom exercises that provide hands-on experience with indexes and abstracting journals keep the students involved. Team teaching can help to hold the classes' attention. There are many ways to organize a class session that will keep the students alert and interested. The best advice to those teaching course-related classes is to experiment with different techniques. Eventually, the best method for each individual will emerge and effective library instruction will be the result.

When planning for course-related library sessions, careful attention should be given to the opening minutes of the class. The proverb that "well begun is half done" is quite applicable here. Every effort must be made to capture and keep the attention of the students. One effective method of accomplishing this is to start with controversial or relevant questions designed to pique the classes' curiosity. For example: "Suppose you want to find information on cohabitation on college campuses? Where would you look? I can tell you how to find ten books and articles on the subject in less than ten minutes." Or: "Let's say you have a job interview with Texas Instruments. Do you know how to find out about the company's products, legal entanglements, financial health, current research, personnel policies, executives and directors?" David Peele's article, "The Hook Principle," is a humorous, thought-provoking description of this technique of catching and holding the interest of a class.[3]

Another way to begin is to tell the class who you are. Write your name, office, and telephone number on the blackboard so they will be able to find you again. You may want to say a few words about your background, your job, other experience you have had (especially if it is relevant to the subject you are teaching), whether you have taught this course before, and any other information that is pertinent or may interest them.

Then find out who they are. The questions asked will depend upon what is already known about this group of students and what the session is intended to accomplish. A group of upper-level students in a business writing course might be asked, for example, "How many of you have completed the library skills workbook?" "How do you locate periodicals in this library?" "How many of you are familiar with the *Readers' Guide to Periodical Literature* [hold up a copy to help them identify it] and the *Business Periodicals Index* [hold up sample]?" "How many of you are accounting majors? Marketing? Management? Other? What is your major?"

The number and scope of the questions asked will depend on how much is known beforehand about the class, and how the students respond to the questions. Questions can be used throughout the session as a means of maintaining interest and getting responses. A student's description of how he or she has used a particular reference work is often worth more than a lengthy description of that work by a librarian.

Once you have the students' attention and have learned something about them, it is helpful to let them know what to expect of the remaining fifty to fifty-five minutes of the session. Many teachers write a brief outline on the blackboard or include it in a handout. Some briefly explain to the students how the remaining time will be divided. It is also helpful to explain the purpose of the library session. How will the information they are about to acquire be useful to them in the present course, in the rest of their academic careers, and in the "real" world? It is important for the librarian to keep the needs of the students foremost at all times. If this is done, the students will also see the relevance of each topic discussed in the library session, and their level of interest will remain high.

It is difficult to know exactly how much material to include in a one-hour session, and how much time to spend on each topic. Sara Lou Whildin's article in the 1975 *Drexel Library Quarterly* contains some pungent observations on this matter which are useful to any instructional librarian in danger of losing perspective.[4] It is usually better to simplify as much as possible, covering a few essentials carefully and thoroughly, rather than to encourage the students to swallow a complete smorgasbord. While an extensive array of information and materials may be indicated by means of bibliographies or other handouts, judicious sampling of a few choice morsels will avoid indigestion.

Among the essentials, a discussion of a few helpful techniques for using the subject card catalog is usually in order. Even in advanced classes, there is seldom an awareness of the *Library of Congress Subject Headings* list. If some of the students are familiar with the books, ask for a description of how they used them. If a list of assigned topics is available, this is an ideal place to select one or two examples to show how the subject-headings volumes can be helpful. Mentioning such examples as "European War, 1914-1918" versus "World War I," or explaining why one must look for books on babies under the subject heading "infants," may also be helpful. A word about how the immense size and complexity of the Library of Congress holdings makes change slow and difficult can help students understand why the system is as unwieldy as it is. This might also be the place for a brief discussion of the problems that result from different names different people call things; suggestions can be elicited from the group. In certain subject fields there are particularly thorny problems which should be explained if the students are working in these areas. It is often helpful to either include sample sections from the *LCSH* with other handouts, or show a sample page on a transparency, opaque projector, or slide. You may wish to provide a list of appropriate subject headings for the particular discipline covered by the course, or for selected topics the students have chosen. You may wish to add that these subject headings can also be useful in determining terminology to search under in various indexes and abstracts.

Students usually see the difficulties they encounter with the subject arrangement of the card catalog more positively when they realize the limitations of the system, the difficulties anyone would have in assigning subject headings, and the promise of improvement held out by computerization. The nature of the card catalog may be analogous to that which prompted Winston Churchill's assessment of democracy as "the worst system devised by the wit of man, except for all the others."[5]

A second essential item is a discussion of selected indexes and abstracts. Depending on the students' assigned topics and the nature of the class, it may be helpful to provide appropriate subject headings for each index. Mentioning the strong points of a few of the indexes and explaining the differences between an index and an abstract is often useful. The similarity in format of all the Wilson indexes might be stressed: "If you can use the *Readers' Guide,* you can use this." The *Readers' Guide* makes a good starting point for discussion, as nearly every student is familiar with it. Unfortunately, an astounding number of students believe that every periodical in the library is indexed in the *Readers' Guide.* Depending on the level of the class, an explanation of why it is expeditious to use an index rather than sort through periodicals issue by issue, may be in line. In other instances it may be wise to stress ways of finding out what periodicals a particular index covers, where a particular periodical is indexed, and how to decipher abbreviations. Thesauri, such as those for *Psychological Abstracts* and *ERIC,* can usually be dispensed with quickly by comparing them to the *Library of Congress Subject Headings.* Avoid too much detailed explanation concerning indexes and abstracts. The best way for students to learn the details is through hands-on experience. By accumulating enough discarded copies of monthly or quarterly issues of indexes and abstracts it is possible to incorporate an exercise into the class activities. It is also possible to use the printed guides and samples available from various indexing and abstracting services. Save breath and class time by letting them learn by doing.

A third item that bears mentioning, this one especially in relationship to the "search strategy," is the technique necessary for obtaining access to background material, especially specialized encyclopedias and handbooks. Selected specialized encyclopedias and handbooks may be mentioned, with a note on how to locate others through the card catalog or guides to the literature. Have some sample volumes available to show the class.

In almost any session, some mention of a few general reference works such as almanacs, biographical dictionaries, and statistics sources is necessary. In addition, there are usually a few tools pertaining to a particular discipline that should be singled out. These should be carefully selected to match the needs of the course. There is no general agreement among librarians as to the appropriateness of introducing students to such "librarians' tools" as Sheehy and Walford. If the class is especially interested in particular types of information or a certain aspect of reference materials, take the opportunity to expand. Add a few authors and titles on the spot to supplement the prepared bibliography. On the other hand, if the students' interest shows signs of waning, skip some of the material you intended to cover and make an effort to inject new energy and enthusiasm into the next segment of the presentation.

It is in the discussion of reference works that librarians are most prone to be bogged down. Every potentially helpful source simply cannot be covered. It is wise to limit the discussion to a few distinctive books, emphasizing that many more exist and students should (1) ask a librarian for help, (2) consult certain subject headings in the card catalog, (3) browse near that same call number on the reference shelves for more material of the same kind, or (4) consult a guide—either general (e.g., Sheehy) or specialized (e.g., Bell's *A Guide to Library Research in Psychology*)—in order to locate others.

The course-related session often includes a sample search. There are several ways to handle this. One is to ask the students to select a topic on the spot, while the librarian impressively improvises a search. Another technique is to select one of the students' topics or a similar topic and actually conduct a thorough search beforehand. This can be effective in bringing the librarian closer to the students' perspective, and can also be a valuable learning experience for the librarian, especially if the subject is one with which he or she is not especially familiar. This method enables the librarian to give the students a blow-by-blow account of the struggles involved in a successful search. Mentioning specific details, problems encountered, and surprising discoveries all add realism and interest to the lecture. It helps to view the search in epic terms. Every searcher is in fact a Ulysses or a Beowulf, if not resisting Sirens and slaying dragons, at least overcoming incredible obstacles to achieve a goal. It is possible to coordinate the use of slides or transparencies with the presentation of a prepared search. Some librarians have also developed slide-tape presentations which follow a search strategy format. Any of these techniques adds variety to the one-hour presentation, and provides a change of pace for the librarian as well as for the students. Point-of-use slide-tape programs designed to explain particular reference works such as *Psychological Abstracts* or *Social Sciences Citation Index* might also be incorporated into the presentation.

A fitting close to the course-related session is an in-class exercise. The easiest type of exercise to use in class, and often the most beneficial, is one requiring the use of indexes and abstracts. There are many varieties of exercises. The students can look up suggested topics or be allowed to choose their own. They can be required to use the same index or be given a choice of indexes and abstracts. It may be possible to complete the exercise entirely within the classroom if there is an extensive collection of duplicate materials available, or in the reference area if there is not. It is also possible to design exercises requiring that students use the card catalog, locate a volume in the stacks, and make use of various reference works. However, this usually requires more time than is available in one course-related session—especially in a large library.

Although they are time-consuming, exercises are important in reinforcing the learning acquired through lectures and discussion. They also lead the student logically into the course project or assignment. By saving them for last, they can be finished outside of class if necessary. Those who finish quickly will be free to leave, and those who take longer or have many questions can take the time they need without holding up the others. In some cases the instructor will ask the students to return the exercises at the next class session. More extensive exercises could also be designed to be evaluated by either the instructor or the librarian and count toward the student's grade in the course, perhaps as a preliminary step in the completion of a paper. Some sample exercises are appended to this chapter.

SUMMARY

The foregoing elements of the course-related session have been discussed in an order in which they are frequently presented. Even in a session as short as one hour, varying the pace and type of activity keeps the interest level high. Scheduling three different types of activity within an hour often works well. These could be a lecture/discussion, an audiovisual presentation, and an exercise. Or one could prepare a lecture followed by a search presentation followed by an exercise.

There are, of course, many variations in methods of presentation. A perusal of some of the articles listed under "teaching techniques" in the *ERIC* abstracts may uncover fresh ideas. New ideas are also constantly encountered at conferences, in library instruction literature, and through communication with colleagues. In order to avoid becoming bored with a routine and in turn boring the students, the teacher of course-related library instruction sessions must constantly be alert to ways to vary and improve his or her presentation.

MATERIALS AND EQUIPMENT

Because the course-related session is so concentrated, the use of media can greatly enhance the presentation in the manner of "a picture is worth a thousand words." Among materials most frequently used are transparencies, slides, slide-tape programs, videotapes, giant-size catalog cards, and various handouts such as worksheets and bibliographies. Reference works and other books and periodicals may also be utilized, as well as samples of various microforms.

Sample subject headings, index entries, and catalog cards can be shown by using transparencies, slides, posters, and handouts. The advantage of the large format is that specific features can be pointed to and easily seen by all. On the other hand, the handouts are often easier to prepare. They also allow space for the students to write notes and comments, and give them something to take away for future reference.

Holding up a copy of a book, opening it to illustrate the arrangement inside, and passing it around the classroom can help imprint it in the students' memories, as long as such a practice is not overdone. In fact, such activity can become a distraction if students are looking at the books being passed rather than listening to the lecture.

Interesting examples of books and periodicals pertaining to the students' subject area can be shown, with a mention of how they were located. Such a method can also be incorporated into a slide-tape program. The demonstration of some of the kinds of materials the library has on particular topics can be especially helpful in the case of items such as government documents or maps whose nature may not be fully understood. Books and periodicals can also be set up in a display which students can look at after class.

Presenting samples of varieties of microforms and passing them around for students to handle, provides many students with their first actual contact with these materials. It is also possible to demonstrate the use of fiche or film readers in the classroom and provide time at the end of the session for "hands-on" experience.

Effective use of any materials requires thorough preparation. The librarian must control the materials, not vice versa. A person who is all thumbs at the thought of setting up a synchronized slide-tape program with projector, tape recorder, and screen, should not attempt such a feat without plenty of practice or the presence of a thoroughly prepared assistant. Even holding up books and posters must be done carefully and with proper pacing.

There are several ways to simplify handling materials and equipment. If several librarians are teaching sections of the same course, all can work together, sharing the development of materials and the gathering of books and equipment. A collection of discarded indexes and reference books kept in or near the classroom makes these easy to gather. A centrally located file of bibliographies, worksheets, withdrawn microforms, catalog card samples, posters, transparencies, and handouts—ideally, supervised by a secretary—makes these materials available to all and prevents unnecessary duplication. Although preparation of various media requires extra effort, the resulting lively, polished, and tightly organized presentation often makes such efforts worthwhile.

EVALUATION OF COURSE-RELATED INSTRUCTION

Evaluation of course-related library sessions can be accomplished in a variety of ways. The most informal of these methods is observation. A class which up to this term has had obvious difficulty with a library assignment, no longer shows up at the reference desk. Students bring bibliographies, handouts, and topical guides to the library and make use of them. Those students who seem to be using reference materials well can be asked if they have been involved in a course-related session.

It may also be desirable to use more formal methods. It is always possible to use pretests and posttests to check for improvement. This approach will be testing skills and recall. For feedback on students' attitudes toward the class session, a questionnaire can be sent to the class toward the end of the term. Students can be queried on whether they feel the library session helped them with their assignments. Another, and probably more valuable, evaluation method could be termed "interaction." The librarian teams with the faculty member and evaluates the students' term papers, including the outline of the initial literature search, the final bibliography, and/or the entire paper. The librarian is able to evaluate how well certain materials were used, as well as comment on key research material the student may have missed. Such involvement provides direct feedback to the librarian about the way students have used the material presented in the course-related session.

Faculty response should be requested. Did the library session fit the goals and objectives of the course? Was there any noticeable improvement in the quality of the term papers? Should the library session be included the next time the class is taught? Should the session be scheduled earlier or later in the term?

It may be useful to use a combination of evaluation methods. Sampling techniques can be used so that it isn't necessary to test or question every class every term. With direct feedback from faculty and students, course-related sessions can be improved and strengthened. Ineffective instruction wastes the time of all who are involved.

FOOTNOTES

1. "On Sangamon State University," *The Journal of Academic Librarianship* 1: 3 (September 1975).
2. Conversation with Bruce Sajdak, Instructional Librarian, Undergraduate Library, University of Maryland.
3. David Peele, "The Hook Principle," *RQ* 13: 135-138 (Winter 1973).
4. Sara Lou Whildin, "Plimpton Prepares: How to Win the Library Instruction Game," *Drexel Library Quarterly* 8: 231-235 (July 1972).
5. Laurence J. Peter, *Peter's Quotations: Ideas for Our Times* (New York: Morrow, 1977), p. 157.

SUGGESTED READINGS

Breivik, Patricia Senn. "Leadership, Management, and the Teaching Library." *Library Journal* 103 (October 15, 1978): 2,045-2,048.

Farber, Evan, et al. "An Intrinsic Instruction Activity: Course-Related Programs for Subject Majors," in Carolyn A. Kirkendall, ed., *Putting Library Instruction in Its Place: In the Library and in the Library School,* pp. 37-52. Ann Arbor: Pierian, 1978.

Frick, Elizabeth, "Information Structure and Bibliographic Instruction." *The Journal of Academic Librarianship* 1 (September 1975): 12-14.

Hardesty, Larry, Lovrich, Nicholas P., Jr., and Mannon, James. "Evaluating Library-Use Instruction." *College and Research Libraries* 40 (July 1979): 309-317.

Kennedy, James. "Integrated Library Instruction." *Library Journal* 95 (April 15, 1970): 1,450-1,453.

Kennedy, James. "Question: A Separate Course in Bibliography or Course-Related Library Instruction?" in Sul H. Lee, ed., *Library Orientation,* pp. 18-28. Ann Arbor: Pierian, 1972.

Kirk, Thomas, "Course-Related Library Instruction in the 1970's," in Hannelore B. Rader, ed., *Library Instruction in the Seventies: State of the Art,* pp. 35-46. Ann Arbor: Pierian, 1977.

Peele, David. "The Hook Principle." *RQ* 13 (Winter 1973): 135-138.

Whildin, Sara Lou. "Plimpton Prepares: How to Win the Library Instruction Game." *Drexel Library Quarterly* 8 (July 1972): 231-235.

CHAPTER 5

Library Skills Workbooks

BACKGROUND

The concept of the workbook or exercise book has been around for many years. Many texts used in elementary, secondary, and postsecondary schools are accompanied by exercises which provide the student with the opportunity to write or experience the textual content. The questions are designed to guide the thinking of the students who are completing them. Laboratory manuals used for chemistry and physics are excellent examples of such text supplements.

The library workbook is a specialized combination of text and exercises centering on the holdings of an individual library. It is often written, produced, and distributed in-house. Specific locations and call numbers are included in the workbook. The recent popularity of library workbooks at the postsecondary level can be traced to Miriam Dudley's efforts in the undergraduate library at University of California, Los Angeles.[1,2] In the late sixties, Dudley developed a library workbook for use in a special program for minority students. The original book has been modified and revised over the years and is presently in use at UCLA's College Library for a variety of undergraduate classes.

This same book has served as a model for many library workbooks in existence today. Over the years, interest in the workbook approach to library instruction has grown. Larger institutions are able to use the workbook to reach large numbers of students in a relatively simple way. There is very little investment of staff time, compared to credit and course-related instruction, and yet 4,000 to 5,000 students per year are able to receive basic library instruction. Some smaller libraries have opted to use the workbook approach because it frees the few individuals already doing instruction to concentrate on upper-level courses and other activities. The staffs at these smaller libraries feel that the workbook is able to meet the needs of their students. A partial listing of those academic libraries using a workbook approach is included at the end of this chapter.[3]

What advantage is such a program to the student? First of all, it is self-paced, thus allowing for individual differences. Since it is an unstructured assignment, students may fit it into their schedules when they wish. They may decide to complete a chapter a day or finish it all at once. They also have the opportunity to work with the indexes, reference books, serials listings, and the card catalog, thus reinforcing what they have read. Finally, the sad fact is that this may be the only activity that provides formal library instruction in the entire academic career of the student.

ADVANCED SUBJECT WORKBOOKS

Although the discussion up to this point has centered on beginning-level workbooks, advanced workbooks have been and are being developed by librarians in specialized subject areas such as business, the humanities, the social sciences, and the sciences. Also The Libraryworks, a division of Neal-Schuman Publishers, has published advanced workbooks in history, political science, sociology, and business management, and other books are planned for the areas of anthropology, geography, economics, psychology, communication, law, music, education, and philosophy.[4] Generally the subject-oriented workbooks are used with appropriate courses from specific departments outside of the library. Although there will be no further discussion of advanced-subject workbooks, the considerations involved in putting together a beginning-level workbook are quite appropriate for the subject workbook.

FINDING A PLACE FOR A WORKBOOK PROGRAM

There are a variety of ways that workbooks can fit into the overall curriculum plan of the college or university. The most common method is to attach a workbook requirement to an already existing course. It is important to decide how the workbook program will be used. Is it intended to reach all beginning students or is it to be used by selected classes as faculty needs dictate? For example, one professor from Social Sciences 100 decides that the workbook would be a very good project that fits in with the goals of his or her class. The professor then makes arrangements with the library to manage the program for the class. The library does not attempt to see that all other sections of Social Sciences 100 become involved in the program.

On the other hand, if the basic objective of establishing a workbook program is to reach all beginning library users, it becomes necessary to make it part of a course that is required in all baccalaureate programs. Basic English classes have often been chosen for this reason. However, consideration should be given to such courses as speech communication and the social sciences.

This latter approach is far from ideal. In the aftermath of the 1960s, academic curriculums changed radically. Although Harvard, a leader in educational trends, has recently returned to a required core curriculum, many academic institutions still have a minimal number of required courses. Students are given the flexibility of shaping a curriculum that meets their needs and interests. Without a core curriculum or basic degree requirement, it becomes difficult to cover all freshmen. Also, even if there are required courses, the library's program is at the mercy of the peaks and valleys of course enrollment, as well as the enthusiastic or lackadaisical attitudes of the faculty teaching the classes.

Another weakness of attaching the workbook to a beginning-level course is the failure to reach transfer students. Some academic institutions depend heavily on upper-division transfers. Many large state-supported universities absorb students from state-supported two-year colleges. This group of students will be missed by a program administered in the basic lower-division courses. Some institutions, such as Penn State, have required the workbook in the basic English class at its branch campuses as well as at the main campus, yet this still does not meet the needs of those students transferring from other institutions.

Another method of integrating the workbook program into the curriculum is to offer it as a credit course, usually for one credit. It could be required for all students before graduation, it could be an elective, or a course that could be used to fulfill one of the degree requirements. Although the credit structure sounds ideal, there are many obstacles to overcome. First of all, establishing any credit program in an academic institution is not simple. There are curriculum review committees which discuss, screen, accept, reject, or recommend new courses. A credit course must meet established criteria. For example, for each credit offered, there is normally an accountability for hours and lab periods that the class must meet. A self-paced program such as the workbook may not be acceptable under such standards. In addition, the establishment of a credit course as a basic degree requirement brings every academic department into the picture. This one credit could change the total number of hours needed for all graduates, whether in engineering, business, science, or any other major. Departments tend to be very sensitive about such things. Furthermore, some libraries do not belong to an academic unit and are therefore not able to offer courses. Any such library wishing to offer the workbook as a course would need to find an academic home for it, most likely in the liberal arts area.

IMPLEMENTING THE WORKBOOK PROGRAM

A workbook program is not a small activity that can be accomplished in a librarian's spare time. It needs to be planned carefully, with much thought given to details. Here is a list of some of the questions that should be answered before taking any steps toward implementation:

1. How many students will be involved?
2. Where will it fit into the curriculum? (credit, attached to class, on demand)
3. What term will it begin?
4. How will the books be printed?
5. Where will the books be sold?
6. What areas of the library will be involved?
7. Will there be a pilot program?
8. How much will the program cost?
   a. salary/staff time
   b. printing
   c. duplicate library resources
   d. photoduplication
9. Can the program pay for itself?

It may be beneficial to read an article entitled "A Self-Paced Workbook Program for Beginning College Students."[5] This will provide some background and information on the costs of an existing program.

When the appropriate information is gathered and analyzed, the library administration should be approached with the proposal for a workbook program. It is important to be well informed and to remain open to all questions and suggestions. Administrators have perspectives different from those of a reference or instructional librarian, and they can often anticipate problems not within the scope of the person planning the program. Also, seed money will be needed to begin the program, and the budget office must be aware of what this will involve and how it will affect the library budget.

It is highly recommended that there be a pilot program lasting from six months to a year. This should definitely be carried out if a credit structure is being planned. This time period will allow the library to evaluate its commitment to the project before the program becomes locked into the curriculum. The pilot period will also allow time to work out the "bugs" that inevitably show up in new projects. The door should be left open either to retain or drop the program at the end of the trial period.

Besides library administrators, it is essential to interact with other professionals and staff in the library. The workbook concept should be thoroughly discussed and understood. In a small library this may not present a problem, but in a larger library there may be a number of individuals who should be consulted. For example, if the workbook includes a self-guided tour, there will be 100 or 500 or 1,000 students walking through such areas as the card catalog, general reference, maps, documents and so forth. There may be chapters in the workbook on these same areas. It is important for the individuals responsible to be informed and involved, and it may even be desirable to have them write or review the chapters.

A third group that must be approached is the faculty. If a pilot project is being considered, members of the faculty who have shown support for the library or library instruction can be asked to participate. Strong support may also be found among basic-skills instructors. If a certain course, such as English composition, is the eventual target, it is wise to make inroads with some faculty members during the pilot period. No matter which courses and which individuals are involved, be open with them. These colleagues can provide valuable feedback and support which will contribute to the success of the program.

Last but not least, heads of the various departments should be aware of the involvement of a course or faculty member in the library project. This may be accomplished through the faculty member or through a group meeting involving key individuals in the program. No matter how it is done, it is vital. Administrators do not enjoy surprises, especially when they affect their departments.

If the decision is to retain the program at the end of the pilot period, paper work should be initiated for a credit structure or departmental commitment. The actual transition from the pilot program to a regular program should be relatively smooth since most of the problems will have been ironed out.

PUTTING TOGETHER A WORKBOOK

Begin by looking at other workbooks.[6] These books can be valuable sources of information and ideas. It should be noted, however, that workbooks fall under the jurisdiction of the copyright law, and they should not be adapted without copyright release.

In looking at the various workbooks, a basic format emerges. There are individual units or chapters which have written descriptions, followed by sets of questions that use the material covered. The following topics are covered in most workbooks: a tour of the library, the card catalog, classification systems, stacks, book reviews, indexes, dictionaries, encyclopedias, almanacs, statistics, and biography. Other units that are dependent on the holdings of a particular library are newspaper indexes, maps, government documents, audiovisual services, and reserve reading. Chapters and units should be chosen that fit the resources of the library where the workbook will be used.

Once the units are decided upon, it is necessary to develop a text. This can be accomplished in two ways. The first is to write the text yourself. The descriptions included in each chapter can be very specific as to the holdings and services of an individual library. The second, and easier, means of developing a text is to use or adapt material already developed (don't forget copyright release). This has the advantage of saving time and effort.

No matter which method is used in developing the textual portion of the workbook, there are two important points to remember: accuracy and readability. Descriptions of departments, reference books, the card catalog, and library services should be accurate. Making a statement such as "The card catalog provides access to all library material" can be dangerously misleading. Does it take into account vertical file material, uncataloged government documents, or maps? Each statement should be closely examined for inaccuracies. If the workbook is being adapted from one already developed, there is a need for extra caution. What is accurate in one library may not be in another. It may be beneficial to have the various chapters written or reviewed by individuals from other areas of the library. For example, the unit on government documents could be the responsibility of the documents staff.

Readability is the second important point to consider in writing the text. This is comprised of a combination of elements. First, the grammar, punctuation, and sentence structure should be correct. Even though the book is developed in-house, there isn't any excuse for poor writing. A good editor can be helpful. A second element of readability is clarity. Concepts and ideas should be clearly described, and library jargon should be avoided. The examples used with the text should be interesting, clear, and relevant. Finally, a reading level should be established that meets the reading and comprehension skills of those who will be using the book. Vocabulary and text that are beyond the ability of the students will be the cause of much frustration. Students should be able to read the text, understand what is being discussed, and be ready to answer questions about the material.

Once the text has been written, edited, and checked for accuracy, it is ready for the typist. The printing method will determine how the typing is to be done. If the workbook will be run off on a mimeograph machine, it will be necessary to have the typing done on stencils. If the book is going to be typeset by a printer, a good paper copy may be sufficient. When the typist finishes, the pages should be proofread. Even one tiny error in a crucial spot can cause much grief. It is important to catch the mistakes before printing.

After writing the text, the next step is to develop the questions to accompany each unit. The main purpose of the workbook is to provide hands-on experience with library materials. The questions that are developed for each unit require the students to use the material discussed. This provides reinforcement of the textual portion.

Workbooks from other libraries may be helpful in deciding what type of questions could be asked. Here are samples from two units:

1. Card Catalog
   A. Who wrote the book ___Helping Others (HV91 .H26)___?
   B. ___John Alton___ wrote a book assigned the call number ___TR850 .A54___. What is its title?

2. Dictionaries
   A. Using any of the general English-language dictionaries, find the meaning of the word ___gallinaceous___.
   B. Look up the same word you just used in the *Oxford English Dictionary.* Who used this word in a quotation in ___1802___?

For students to answer these questions it is necessary for them to use the card catalog, a general English-language dictionary, and the *Oxford English Dictionary* respectively. Similar questions developed for other units also require students to handle the library material being discussed in the text.

Here are a few examples of other possible questions:

3. Maps
   A. For a class assignment, you have been assigned to find some information about Kettering, Ohio Using the *Rand McNally Atlas and Commercial Guide,* answer the following questions:
      1) In which county is the town located?
      2) What is the elevation of the town?
      3) What is the population listed?

4. Government Documents
   A. The 1967 *Monthly Catalog* lists a government publication on witches' broom disease.
      1) What is the entry number for this publication?
      2) What is the Superintendent of Documents number for this publication?
      3) Which U.S. Government agency issued this publication?

5. Encyclopedias
   A. Using the *Collier's Encyclopedia* find out: Who was Quintus of Smyrna ?

6. Classification Systems
   A. With what letters do call numbers of books on Chemistry begin?
   B. A call number beginning with the letters HG will cover what subject?

If every student in a class were given a self-paced library workbook and each workbook had exactly the same questions, a serious problem could develop: students might copy one another's answers. To avoid this, different sets of questions are developed. In the examples just listed, there are portions of the questions that can be changed. Instead of looking up the town of "Kettering, Ohio" in example #3, the student could be asked to look up "Beckley, West Virginia" or "Aliquippa, Pennsylvania." The basic idea is to have the same textual portions for everyone, but to have different exercise sets.

This means that someone must develop not only the questions, but also variations for the questions. To clarify this, let's say that it is decided that every student will be asked the following almanac question:

What baseball team won the________League Penant in______?

To vary this question, the words "American" or "National" would be used in the first blank and a year would be added in the second blank. So Student A would be asked which team won the __American__ League Penant in __1948__, and Student B would be asked which team won the__National__League Penant in__1961__. There can be many variations for the same question, thus making each student's workbook unique.

Besides controlling copying, varying the questions has one additional advantage. Spreading the questions out prevents excessive wear and tear on the library materials. If, for example, 1,000 students look up exactly the same word in a dictionary, that page will not survive long. If, however, there are 100 different words to be looked up, each page is used by only ten of the 1,000 students.

Format for the Questions and Answers

The appearance of the question page has changed over the years. Originally, in the UCLA workbook and others like it, the individual questions were hand copied by the staff into the blanks. For example, every book looked like the following:

Who won the Pulitzer Prize for________in ______?

The staff would write in longhand the word Fiction, History, Biography, and so forth and then a year—1950, 1963, 1972, and so on. A master question-and-answer set was kept for each book, and this was used to prepare as well as correct the workbooks. In an effort to save staff time, some libraries had the students themselves fill in the question blanks. A librarian would go to the classroom and pass out one book and one master set of questions to each student. The students would transfer the questions from the master set to the blanks in their own workbooks. The librarian would collect the master sets and each student now had a unique workbook. Another method was to staple the questions to the back cover of each book and refer students to them at appropriate points in the text.

In an attempt to eliminate the hand preparation of each workbook, a new method was implemented. Typists now prepare the exercise pages as well as the master copy of the text of the workbook. For example, if it is decided that there are to be fifty variations of each question, the typist will first type one stencil or master copy of the exercise page for each chapter, leaving the appropriate blanks in each question. Fifty copies of this exercise page will then be made, after which the typist will fill in the blanks with the different versions of the same question. The result will be fifty master copies of the questions for Chapter One, fifty for Chapter Two, fifty for Chapter Three, and so on. Eventually each chapter will have fifty different sheets of typed questions. By taking one typed question sheet from each chapter pile, a complete set of exercise pages can be collated for each of the fifty workbooks.

Once the text and the question sets are typed, proofread, and corrected, they are ready for printing. If 1,000 workbooks are to be printed, 1,000 copies are made from each stencil or master copy of the text. Only twenty copies will be made from each page of the exercise sets (20 copies × 50 exercise sets = 1,000 workbooks). When the workbooks are collated, the first 20 workbooks have the same questions. The next 20 books are collated with the same textual pages, but include the questions from the next exercise set.

It is important to keep track of which books have which

exercise sets. This is essential for correction purposes. From past experience, it is not recommended that the books be visually coded. This type of marking alerts students to which exercise set their books contain. The more enterprising student will attempt to track down other students with the same workbook. The easiest control method is to use an internal coding system. No marks are put on the workbooks. Rather, a single question within the book serves as the key. For example, let's say that every workbook has the following question:

Looking in *Who's Who in America,* find the birthdate for__________.

Exercise set 1: Ralph Nader
Exercise set 2: Jane Fonda
Exercise set 3: Barbara Jordan
Exercise set 4: William F. Buckley
.
.
.
Exercise set 50: Kurt Vonnegut, Jr.

On a separate piece of paper, all fifty names should be arranged alphabetically. The appropriate set number should be listed next to the names. For example, by using the names above, the list would look like this:

NAME	EXERCISE SET NUMBER
Buckley, William F.	4
Fonda, Jane	2
Jordan, Barbara	3
Nader, Ralph	1
Vonnegut, Kurt Jr.	50

By consulting this list, the person correcting the workbook can tell that the student having to look up "William F. Buckley" has a workbook that uses exercise set 4. The students, meanwhile, cannot tell the workbooks apart. It should be noted that almost any question may be chosen for coding purposes.

At the same time that the preparation method was changed from hand-written to typed, a change was also made in the answer format. In order to reduce correction time, the fill-in-the-blanks format was changed to multiple choice. As the typists filled in the blanks of the exercise sheets, they also typed in the multiple-choice answers. The following is a typical example of such a format:

> Using the appropriate foreign language-English dictionary, give the meaning of the ___French___ word ___soubrette___.
>
> a. lady's maid
> b. a clown
> c. soup
> d. hair ribbon

The student circles the correct answer (a), rather than writing it in an answer blank.

If a multiple-choice format is used, it is necessary to provide an answer key for each exercise set. If there are fifty editions of the workbook, there would be fifty different answer sequences. For example, the answer sequence for Book 1 could look like this: 1. A; 2. D; 3. A; 4. B; 5. C; . . . The answer sequence for Book 2 would be different. It might look like this: 1. B; 2. A; 3. C; 4. C; 5. E; . . . The person correcting each book must first know which book is being corrected and then know the proper answer sequence. So it becomes necessary to keep track of which workbooks have what answer sequences.

Since it can be very time consuming as well as confusing to keep track of fifty or one hundred different answer keys, it becomes desirable to simplify this system. It is possible to use exactly the same answer sequence for more than one workbook. For example, the Penn State workbook has one hundred different exercise sets, but there are only ten different answer sequences. Workbooks 1 through 10 have different exercise sets and different answers, but the *answer sequences* are exactly the same. So whether a student has Workbook 1 or Workbook 6 or Workbook 9, the answer sequence is: 1. B; 2. C; 3. D; 4. A; 5. B; . . . To further illustrate:

WORKBOOK 1

1) What is the title of the book written by __Edmund Jaeger__ with the call number __QH188 .J3__?
    - a. Good Man Fallen Among Fabians
    - (b.) The North American Deserts
    - c. Junks of Central China
2) Who wrote the book entitled __Experimentation in Marketing__ with the call number __HF5415 .2 .B3__?
    - a. Brian Meriman
    - b. Cecily Mackworth
    - (c.) Seymour Banks

WORKBOOK 2

1) What is the title of the book written by __Robert O. Hahn__ with the call number __LB1607 .H16__?
    - a. Urban-Rural Conflict
    - (b.) Creative Teachers: Who Wants Them?
    - c. North Africa: Nationalism to Nationhood
2) Who wrote the book entitled __Suffragettes International__ with the call number __HQ1154 .L58__?
    - a. Ada Nisbet
    - b. Paul Lewis
    - (c.) Trevor Lloyd

The concept of having a limited number of answer sequences simplifies the correction process. Also, it eventually becomes desirable to revise and change the exercise sheets. If the answer sequences are the same, the exercise sheets can be interchanged. This shuffling process allows for multiple variations of the exercise sheets.

WORKBOOK CORRECTIONS

How the workbooks are corrected is directly tied to the type of answer required from the student. If the questions are open ended (fill-in-the-blanks), each answer must be hand corrected. The strong argument for using the fill-in-the-blank format is the fact that the students must think about their answers instead of being guided by the multiple choices listed. For the corrector these open-ended questions can mean a variety of acceptable answers, especially to ambiguous questions. Legibility can also be a problem, for not all students write clearly.

The correction process for the fill-in-the-blanks workbooks can be quite time consuming. It may take five to ten minutes per book, and often it is not realistic to expect that librarians or staff will have hours to devote to corrections. With the multiple-choice format, corrections can be completed very quickly. Also, since there isn't the ambiguity of the open-ended questions, the workbooks can be corrected by anyone with the answer keys. Work-study or wage-payroll students can be utilized in this capacity, and this frees other members of the library staff.

The easiest way to deal with the multiple-choice format is to have the students completing their workbook, transfer their answers to a machine-readable answer form. Most students are well acquainted with this process and need little help or direction in filling out the sheet. When the workbook is corrected and returned to the student, the answer sheet can be kept in the library to serve as a permanent record that the student has completed the workbook requirement. A sample answer form is shown on the opposite page.

Machine-readable answer forms can be corrected by the use of a hand grid or by an optical scanning machine. A hand grid is simply a blank answer sheet with the appropriate holes punched out where the correct answer would normally be filled in with #2 pencil. When the punched-out answer form is placed on top of a student's answer sheet, any incorrect answers can be seen immediately. An optical scanner is a machine that can "read" the correct and incorrect answers by means of a light system. Many colleges and universities have at least one optical scanner, usually in a central testing office. The main disadvantage to using such

NAME ______ COURSE ______ INSTRUCTOR ______ DATE ______

STUDENT NUMBER

TEST FORM (A) (B) (C) (D) (E)

SPECIAL CODE (0) (1) (2) (3) (4) (5) (6) (7) (8) (9)

SEC. NO | A | B | C | D | SCORE

1 (A) (B) (C) (D) (E)
2 (A) (B) (C) (D) (E)
3 (A) (B) (C) (D) (E)
4 (A) (B) (C) (D) (E)
5 (A) (B) (C) (D) (E)
6 (A) (B) (C) (D) (E)
7 (A) (B) (C) (D) (E)
8 (A) (B) (C) (D) (E)
9 (A) (B) (C) (D) (E)
10 (A) (B) (C) (D) (E)
11 (A) (B) (C) (D) (E)
12 (A) (B) (C) (D) (E)
13 (A) (B) (C) (D) (E)
14 (A) (B) (C) (D) (E)
15 (A) (B) (C) (D) (E)
16 (A) (B) (C) (D) (E)
17 (A) (B) (C) (D) (E)
18 (A) (B) (C) (D) (E)
19 (A) (B) (C) (D) (E)
20 (A) (B) (C) (D) (E)
21 (A) (B) (C) (D) (E)
22 (A) (B) (C) (D) (E)
23 (A) (B) (C) (D) (E)
24 (A) (B) (C) (D) (E)
25 (A) (B) (C) (D) (E)
26 (A) (B) (C) (D) (E)
27 (A) (B) (C) (D) (E)
28 (A) (B) (C) (D) (E)
29 (A) (B) (C) (D) (E)
30 (A) (B) (C) (D) (E)
31 (A) (B) (C) (D) (E)
32 (A) (B) (C) (D) (E)
33 (A) (B) (C) (D) (E)
34 (A) (B) (C) (D) (E)
35 (A) (B) (C) (D) (E)
36 (A) (B) (C) (D) (E)
37 (A) (B) (C) (D) (E)
38 (A) (B) (C) (D) (E)
39 (A) (B) (C) (D) (E)
40 (A) (B) (C) (D) (E)
41 (A) (B) (C) (D) (E)
42 (A) (B) (C) (D) (E)
43 (A) (B) (C) (D) (E)
44 (A) (B) (C) (D) (E)
45 (A) (B) (C) (D) (E)
46 (A) (B) (C) (D) (E)
47 (A) (B) (C) (D) (E)
48 (A) (B) (C) (D) (E)
49 (A) (B) (C) (D) (E)
50 (A) (B) (C) (D) (E)
51 (A) (B) (C) (D) (E)
52 (A) (B) (C) (D) (E)
53 (A) (B) (C) (D) (E)
54 (A) (B) (C) (D) (E)
55 (A) (B) (C) (D) (E)
56 (A) (B) (C) (D) (E)
57 (A) (B) (C) (D) (E)
58 (A) (B) (C) (D) (E)
59 (A) (B) (C) (D) (E)
60 (A) (B) (C) (D) (E)

TM NCS Trans Optic F4210 5432

a machine is the fact that most scanners are able to print out the total number of right answers or the total number of wrong ones, but do not indicate which answers are wrong. If students must make corrections, a method to find out which questions must be rechecked will be required. Use of a grid can avoid this drawback, and workbook corrections can still be completed in less than a minute.

Before deciding on an answer format, serious consideration should be given to the size of the program and the staff available to correct the books. Hand correcting 100 fill-in-the-blanks workbooks per semester or term may be within reason. However, if there are 800 or 1,000 workbooks to be corrected, such a format may be undesirable. Common sense should prevail.

PRINTING THE WORKBOOK

Aside from salaries, printing is the most expensive aspect of a workbook program and should be carefully investigated. Workbooks can be completely homemade. If there are printing services as part of the library, it may be advantageous to use them. A good stencil can provide 500–1,000 copies of a page. Also, it may be less expensive to have the exercise sets prepared in-house. Remember, if 50 different sets are being used and 1,000 books are to be printed, there will be only 20 workbooks that have the same exercise sheets.

Printers can also provide good advice on publication. They can suggest the least expensive printing method and will help with the layout. They can also recommend types of binding. Printers can do parts of the job—for example, the cover—while the rest of the workbook can be printed within the library. Shopping around is important. Variations in paper and labor costs can greatly affect the printing costs.

It is very important to know how much lead time the printer needs. Some commercial printers require one to two months for the complete job, which may mean that a book must be ready to go to the printer in late June if it's to be ready by September.

PRICING THE WORKBOOK

Careful consideration should be given to the unit price of the workbook. This price depends on a number of variables. First, the printing cost should be determined. This is quite simple if the job is completed by the printer. For example: 1,000 books × $1.50 per book = $1,500 total charge. If the book is being printed and bound within the library, it is necessary to figure paper costs, stencils, copy fees, covers, binding, and so forth.

The next consideration is where the book is to be sold. This may depend on university and college regulations. If it is allowed, the library can sell the books directly to the students. This saves the middleman markup. This also means that the library must be prepared to handle money in either cash or check form, and have someone do the selling. Another way to sell the workbooks is through a bookstore. This usually means that a certain percentage will be tacked on to cover the overhead for the bookstore. The advantage to this method is that the bookstore handles the sales and the library need not concern itself with the problems that can arise.

Additional charges that may or may not be included in the unit price are salaries, book replacement costs, supplies, and additional photoduplication needs. Again, in some universities and colleges there may be restrictions on including program costs in the price of the material. This would mean that any additional expenses over and above printing costs could not be tacked on. Yet if a justifiable additional amount can be included, a workbook program can virtually pay for itself. If, for example, printing cost for each workbook is $1.50 and the workbooks are sold for $1.50, the library recovers only the printing cost. If, however, the workbooks are priced at $5.00 each, the library receives not only the printing cost but an addition $3.50 that could be used to support other costs incurred by the program.

Aside from recovering the program cost through the cost of the workbook, there is the general tuition fund. If the program becomes a credit course, it may have a claim to all or part of the tuition money generated. If it is attached to a separate course, there may be some sharing with the department concerned. If none of these methods for recovering costs is viable, the library administration should be aware that it will be forced to absorb program costs. This may or may not be acceptable.

LIBRARY RESOURCES

Depending on the number of students involved in the program at one time, it may be necessary to consider duplication of material. One set of the indexes or encyclopedias may be sufficient as long as the questions are spread out over several volumes or issues. For example, if there is a question from the *Readers' Guide,* the question may be developed from the volumes covering 1967 to 1977. If there are 50 different exercise sets, only five questions need to be taken from any one volume. This spreads out the wear and tear on the set.

Individual reference tools such as the *World Almanac* or the *Statistical Abstract,* however, usually need to be duplicated. Three to four copies will normally be sufficient to handle most needs. Both of these are relatively inexpensive, and also can be updated with the new edition each year.

Over a period of two years, with 4,000 to 8,000 students involved, there may be a need to rebind some materials. There is no doubt that the materials are handled a good deal. Rebinding costs should be considered as part of the program costs.

There has been considerable discussion and little agreement on where the workbook resources should be placed.

One school of thought strongly supports the theory that the reference material should be kept in its everyday location and the workbook experience be totally realistic. Theoretically this is fine, except for those libraries where much of this material is used as ready reference at the service desk. This means 100, 500, or 1,000 requests for "the almanac" or "the *Statistical Abstract*." It then becomes a survival tactic to have a separate workbook area or have sufficient copies in the reference stacks to avoid the rush at the desk.

At the other end of the spectrum are those who advocate a separate "learning laboratory." The advantage of such a situation is that the workbook students have their own area and do not compete with nonworkbook library users. The laboratory can also make it easy to identify students having problems. There isn't a right or wrong method for handling material location, but it should fit the needs of the students, the library, and the program. A few different methods could be tried during the pilot period. This is all part of smoothing out the program.

Each library establishing a workbook program will end up determining its own needs, but the following comments may help to serve as a guide. There is a need for a professional librarian to direct the workbook program. This should be someone enthusiastic about the project and in a position to direct the program. Normally this has been an instructional or public-service librarian. There has to be recognition by administrators that such a program can absorb a large percentage of time, particularly during the pilot period. Much of this time should be spent away from the distractions of the service desk. Once the program is in operation, the percentage of time invested in the program is dependent on the amount of support staff. If the "workbook librarian" must develop questions, keep all the records, see to the printing, contact the bookstore, talk with new faculty about the program, correct books, and carry out the countless details involved, the total percentage of time needed for the workbook program will remain high. If this person has help from at least one part-time clerical person, many of the details can be delegated, freeing the "workbook librarian" for other activities.

Clerical help is a necessity for the workbook preparation. Someone has to type the text and prepare the exercise sets. This need not necessarily be a clerical worker employed solely for the program. Secretaries from other areas can be called upon. It is highly recommended, however, that there be at least some part-time clerical help attached to the workbook program. If a part-time or full-time secretary cannot be hired for this program, a percentage of a full-time worker's hours might be set aside. If the workbook is published in-house, there may be a need to support this activity. If there is a separate learning laboratory or a workbook desk where books are sold or turned in for corrections, these areas must be staffed. For some of these activities, wage-payroll and work-study student help has been successful. It is important to plan to have sufficient staff. One person is not able to do everything from typing to correcting. Understaffing can quickly undermine what could be a feasible and exciting program.

FOOTNOTES

1. Miriam Dudley, "The State of Library Instruction Credit Courses and the State of the Use of Library Skills Workbooks," in Hannelore B. Rader, *Library Instruction in the Seventies: State of the Art* (Ann Arbor: Pierian, 1977), pp. 79-84.
2. Miriam Dudley, "The Self-paced Library Skills Program at UCLA's College Library," in John Lubans, Jr., ed., *Educating the Library User* (New York: Bowker, 1974), pp. 330-335.
3. Partial listing of colleges and universities using a library workbook:

    University of California, Los Angeles
    University of Wisconsin, Parkside
    University of Arizona
    The Pennsylvania State University
    Northern Virginia Community College
    University of California, Santa Barbara
    West Virginia University

4. The Libraryworks (New York: Neal-Schuman Publishers, Inc.)
    a. *Materials & Methods for History Research*
    b. *Materials & Methods for Political Science Research*
    c. *Materials & Methods for Sociology Research*
    d. *Materials & Methods for Business Management*
5. Beverly L. Renford, "A Self-paced Workbook Program for Beginning College Students," *Journal of Academic Librarianship* 4:200-205 (September 1978).
6. Samples can be borrowed through LOEX or requested directly from the libraries using workbooks. Some of the libraries may charge for copies of their workbooks.

SUGGESTED READINGS

Dudley, Miriam. "A Self-paced Library Skills Program at UCLA's College Library," in John Lubans, Jr., ed., *Educating the Library User,* pp. 330-335. New York: Bowker, 1974.

Dudley, Miriam. "The State of Library Instruction Credit Courses and the State of the Use of Library Skills Workbook," in Hannelore B. Rader, ed., *Library Instruction in the Seventies: State of the Art,* pp. 79-84. Ann Arbor: Pierian Press, 1977.

Mertins, Barbara. "The Self-paced Workbook in Teaching Basic Library Skills," in Barbara Mertins, comp., *Bibliographic Instruction,* pp. 31-40. West Virginia Library Association. Working Conference of the College and University Section. ERIC Educational Document Reproduction Service, 1977. ED 144 582.

Renford, Beverly L. "A Self-paced Workbook Program for Beginning College Students." *Journal of Academic Librarianship* 4 (September 1978): 200-205.

WORKBOOKS AVAILABLE THROUGH ERIC

Basic Library Skills

Workbook. Library Instruction Series (University of Maine, Orono) ED 162 667 (ED 162 664, ED 162 665, and ED 162 666 are also related to program).

Guide to the University of Kentucky Libraries. ED 126 901, pp. 47-170.

A Media-assisted Library Instruction Orientation Program Report (State University of New York at Brockport). ED 134 138, pp. 34–48.

Advanced Subject Workbooks

A Module for Training Library Researchers (educational psychology) (University of Texas at Austin). ED 145 849.

Workbook for Library Research in Psychology. (State University of New York at Buffalo). ED 151 025.

Library Resources in Education. An Introductory Module for Students and Teachers. (State University of New York at Potsdam). ED 124 129.

CHAPTER 6

Credit Instruction

Often overshadowed by the growing interest in course-related instruction, workbook programs, and other newer methods, the separate course in bibliography nevertheless remains a viable means of library instruction. This course has a long and distinguished past. It formed the basis of the very first library instruction movement in the 1870s,[1] and continued to be popular throughout the 1920s and 1930s, as a glance at the literature of that period reveals.

In a 1964 article in *Library Journal* which may have been a harbinger of the recent interest in library instruction, Daniel Core argued for the establishment of separate courses in bibliography.[2] He cited the huge increase in the genre known as "reference materials" in the twentieth century, and the necessity of training people to understand and use the entire system of organized information. He foresaw such programs as resulting in great benefits for both users and librarians, and claimed the present system of reference service to be "costly and inefficient."[3]

In recent years, however, arguments against the separate bibliographic course have predominated. One of the strongest statements is James Kennedy's address at the 1971 LOEX conference.[4] Among his arguments are: 1. Both students and teachers become bored with intrinsically dull subject matter and homework which seems like busy work, partly because it is unrelated to other course work. 2. Separate courses reach only a small number of students. 3. Most students do not feel a need for a course to introduce them to bibliography, at least not until they have chosen majors and are ready for in-depth searching in their particular fields. Kennedy admits that there have been successful credit courses, but seems to feel they are the results of the extraordinary personalities of the teachers, who are the exception, not the rule.

One of the few librarians to publicly support the credit course in recent years is John Bollier.[5] In describing his successful experience at the Yale Divinity School, he cites the overwhelmingly favorable response of students and other faculty to a course designed for graduate theology students. He felt that, in answer to arguments for course-related instruction, no course could spare the minimum of six to ten hours that would be necessary for adequate coverage of such basics as classification systems, subject headings, and the basic reference works in his field. He also asserts that the students' "level of bibliographic sophistication . . . does not depend upon the number of years enrolled in graduate professional studies, but rather upon a conscious effort, or lack thereof, in studying bibliographic methods and resources."[6]

He compares the study of bibliography to the study of a language, pastoral counseling, or preaching. "The student does not acquire proficiency in any of these skills obliquely through studying only in other fields, but directly by studying and practicing in the discipline itself."[7] Bollier does not deny the value of course-integrated instruction, but feels there is a need for both.

Other arguments in favor of the separate course center on the librarian rather than the student. Anne Roberts' study of credit courses in the State University of New York system cites several instances in which the library administration favored the courses as a means for enhancing the librarians' faculty status.[8] Bollier also mentions that as a result of his work in developing and teaching the course he was appointed to the Yale faculty as lecturer. But perhaps more important than status are the librarians' feelings about the level and quality of instruction that they achieve in separate courses compared to course-related sessions. Several of the librarians in Anne Roberts' study cited the feeling of accomplishment and satisfaction that resulted in seeing a group of students through the course from beginning to end. They would test, evaluate, see the students learn and grow, and adjust their teaching techniques accordingly. This is much more difficult to do in one-shot course-related sessions, where treatment of any topic tends to be superficial and there is seldom an opportunity to assist the student who failed to understand.

Anyone who has taught on a regular basis is surely familiar with the difference between the way it feels to appear for an hour or two as "guest lecturer" and the feeling of being responsible for the sustained movement of an entire group from point A to point B over a period of several weeks or months. If the class fails to grasp a key point in the guest lecturer's presentation, it is unfortunate, and such gaps often go unrecognized. The regular instructor is able to present the key points in a variety of ways, making sure that the ideas are grasped.

It is not difficult to refute Kennedy's arguments against credit instruction. The subject matter need not be intrinsically dull. There can be excitement in learning about systems of organizing information, and in learning about specific reference materials and acquiring the skills to use them, even if there is no immediate need for them. In the same way, people delight in learning mathematical systems, languages, history, or chemistry, even though there is no immediate practical application. Everyone, surely, has a streak of curiosity and a desire to know "how to find out," whether there is an immediate, pressing need for a particular bit of information or not. What else explains the popularity of newspaper columns in the Sunday magazine sections which advertise: "Want the facts? Want to learn the truth about prominent personalities? Want informed opinion?" Many of the questions could be answered by any reference librarian or any individual with basic bibliographic skills.

An attempt to design imaginative exercises often pays off. One teacher was pleased to find that the students not only enjoyed the questions, but in fact reported that their friends and roommates had begun asking them, "What do you have to find out this week?" and exclaiming, "You mean you can find stuff like that in the library?"

Libraries and librarians have too long suffered from an image of dullness that needs to be shaken. The only way to convince others that libraries, the information stored in them, the remarkable methods of organizing this information, and the people who know more about the secrets of these systems than anyone else (the librarians) are not dull, is for librarians to first believe it about themselves.

In addition, although the subject matter of a bibliographic skills course can be exciting in and of itself, it easily can be related to other course work. In fact, the good teacher in any discipline frequently relates the topic at hand to instances that are part of the student's experience, and helps the student make connections between theory and application. The student can also be encouraged to develop a bibliographic project which can be used for another course.

As for Kennedy's second objection, that separate courses reach only a small number of students: at present, this is usually true. However, it need not always be the case. As Daniel Gore suggests,[9] it may be a matter of setting priorities and rescheduling librarians' time. Howard W. Dillon describes the system at Sangamon State, where the new library was established as a teaching library.[10] The administrative duties that frequently occupy much of the librarian's time have been taken over by qualified nonfaculty-status staff, and librarians are principally involved in teaching, reference assistance, collection development, and departmental liaison work. Even if providing enough librarians to teach all the students who need the course seems impossible, incorporating such methods as the library-skills workbook, independent study, audiovisual or computer-assisted instruction into the credit course can help to alleviate this problem.

In addition to rearranging librarians' priorities and schedules, changes may need to be made in the college curriculum and the emphasis of certain courses if a larger number of students is to be reached. College and university faculty members must be aware of the importance of library work, and library assignments that demand a certain quality of work must be part of the courses and the entire curriculum if any program of library instruction is to be successful.

Kennedy's third objection, that most students do not feel a need for a course to introduce them to bibliography, can be answered in much the same way as the first. As Gore says, ". . . often the student knows so little of the resources of the library that he is not even aware that he needs help. . . . The reference librarian cannot answer the questions that are not asked, and they may well be more important than the ones that are."[11] The teacher should be able to awaken students' awareness of what they need to know, and one way of doing this is to reveal a hitherto unknown body of knowledge to the students, encouraging a desire to learn in the process. Perhaps now that the 1960s cry for "relevance" has been succeeded by the call to "return to basics," the student will no longer have to express an immediate "need" for a particular skill or type of knowledge before he or she can be encouraged to acquire it.

The problems a library may have in implementing a program of separate courses in library skills have many similarities with the problems English departments have with their basic composition requirements. Both courses are frequently "required" ones which are offered as a service both to the students and the other departments of the university, and as such often create a heavy burden on the offering department. Both courses also require reinforcement from other departments if they are to be effective. The freshman composition instructor often laments that his efforts are in vain unless instructors of other courses also insist that students' papers be literate and grammatical. The librarian also needs reinforcement of the need for library research skills from other departments.

The separate course is not going to solve all problems of library instruction and library use, but it is one means of instruction which should seriously be considered. Its rewards can be great, for students and librarians both. But the successful course requires careful planning, coordination, and a considerable commitment of time and library resources. Knowledge of curriculum design, teaching techniques, and a firm belief in the value of the subject matter to the students is also helpful.

TYPES OF CREDIT COURSES

The discussion thus far has included all types of separate credit courses. Before we proceed it may be helpful to distinguish among them. The most frequent references to credit courses are to the introductory courses in library skills, often labeled "library studies," "introduction to the library," "basic bibliography," "library skills," or "introduction to research." Sometimes these are required courses, and sometimes elective. They may be offered for three or four credits, with class meetings scheduled over an entire semester or term, or they may be short courses, offered for one or two credits, meeting either for a concentrated block of time or spread out over several weeks. These are usually taught by librarians, but are sometimes sponsored by another department or program.

Another type of credit course, which usually does not receive as much opposition as the introductory library skills course, is the advanced course in the bibliography of a particular discipline. Many graduate programs offer courses of this type taught entirely by the faculty of a particular department, with perhaps an occasional lecture by a librarian. Others are sponsored by a department with a librarian doing the teaching; and still others, such as John Bollier's course for graduate theology and divinity students at Yale, are taught and administered entirely by the library. Unfortunately many graduate programs do not offer library research or bibliography courses at all, nor do they seem to feel there is a need for any—whence frequently come the future professors who will also not feel a need for library instruction for their students. Most of the comments in the following sections have been prepared with the introductory course in mind, but many of the statements are also applicable to advanced courses, which, unfortunately, have not been as extensively discussed in library literature.

STEPS IN ESTABLISHING A CREDIT PROGRAM OR COURSE

The first step in establishing a credit is to determine that there is a need for one. This may require some research, but chances are that the college or university already has suitable data available. Such data would include the total number of enrolled students, grade-point averages, majors, special admission programs, and term standings. There is also informative material kept on the various departments and/or colleges. Courses offered, program requirements, and faculty specialization are helpful to have on hand. By using this information a potential audience for credit courses in library skills and research can be identified. Special programs such as Developmental Year or the Honors Program may be excellent target groups. Also, by looking closely at the various program requirements, it may be apparent that a credit course in library skills will not succeed since few students can afford room in their overcrowded schedules for still another class. Any available data that will help to establish a clear picture of the students' needs should be examined.

If after careful deliberation it is decided that the library should be involved in credit courses, the goals and objectives should be established. What is the purpose of such a course or program? What topics and material will it cover? Will it be overlapping with courses already in existence on campus? How will it fit into a particular student's education or major? At this point it is helpful to write up a course or program outline. This will be an essential document for presenting the idea of a credit program or course to the library administration. Also, course outlines are usually required by the various curriculum committees on campus.

Next, it is necessary to determine what the program will cost in terms of personnel, space, and equipment. Who will teach the course? Will another person assume some of the teacher's regular work assignment? Will someone be paid to teach the course? Are there facilities in the library for teaching, or must it be done somewhere else? Is the instructional space shared with those involved in other campus activities? If so, will there be a conflict? Does the librarian have an office in which to hold conferences with students? Is special equipment required—duplicating machines, blackboards, audiovisual equipment, desks, and chairs? Having answers to these questions will be helpful when discussing the possibility of credit instruction with those in authority.

Follow the existing guidelines for the college, university, or library for setting up a course or program. These will vary greatly from institution to institution. If the library has never offered a course before, move very carefully. Gather as much information and talk to as many people inside and outside the library as possible. Contact people at schools with library instruction programs similar to what you have in mind to find out how they did it. There may be university- or college-wide procedures for establishing courses, or there may be individual departmental or divisional policies and guidelines. Learn the policies of the institution and follow them to the letter. Get the help of other people on campus who have experience in setting up new courses or programs.

Some colleges and universities will not allow the library to offer courses. Often library instruction programs at these institutions are sponsored by another division—sometimes the college of education, sometimes the graduate library school, sometimes under some type of basic skills option. Explore all the possibilities. The more contacts made with faculty members outside the library, and the more help elicited from them, the more support they will provide the program when it is underway. Gaining support at the outset, and even being forced to find a home outside of the library for your project, can be a blessing in disguise. Sometimes all that is needed is the wholehearted support of one influential faculty member.

DESIGNING THE COURSE

Once the course proposal has been approved, specific day-by-day details must be completed. First, begin by writing a statement of purpose. Think in terms of what is to be communicated to the students about the course. This is the equivalent of writing a thesis statement. The more thought and care put into it, the better organized the course will be, and the easier it will be to set out the subsequent details. For example: "The purpose of this course is to introduce the student to techniques of library research, through reading, discussion, practical exercises, and the completion of a term bibliography project." This statement includes the what and the how. An even better one might also tackle the "why."

The second step in designing the course is to decide upon its goals and objectives. This may have been completed earlier, when preparing the course proposal, but the goals and objectives should be reviewed and revised. Such listings will determine what material the course will cover and what the students should know by the end of the course.

Once the objectives are set, appropriate teaching methods can be chosen. The teaching methods could include lectures, reading assignments, AV presentations, class exercises, term projects, guest lectures, and so on. More detailed information on these various methods is included later in this chapter.

The final consideration in designing a course is the criteria that will be used for grading and evaluating the students and the course. Frequently the college and university has guidelines in this area. There also may be evaluation forms in existence which can be used. It is a good idea to have a very detailed breakdown of what percentage each class activity contributes to a final grade. Such detail prevents any misunderstanding between the student and the teacher.

When the purpose of the course, the goals and objectives, the teaching methods, and the evaluation procedures are established, everything can be put together and a course syllabus can be organized.

The Syllabus

Sample syllabi for credit courses may be obtained from library instruction clearinghouses. Some of the articles describing specific courses (listed at the end of this chapter) also include course outlines. A well-prepared course description and outline, distributed to the students at the beginning of the term, can be an asset to the course. It lets the students know what to expect and gives them a guide to consult throughout the course.

The amount of detail included in various syllabi varies greatly. The personality of the instructor often determines whether an outline is lengthy or brief, detailed or general. Many instructors find it helpful to plan the course as carefully as possible at the beginning, while others prefer to allow for maximum flexibility.

Some general guidelines, with samples of types of information which might be included, follow:

1. Official name and number of the course. It is also wise to include the name of the college or university, perhaps by having the syllabus prepared on letterhead paper. A disap-

pointing number of syllabi received from clearinghouses are not identified by school.

2. Additional descriptive name of the course. For example: the official name may be General Studies 101, while the descriptive name is "Introduction to the Library."

3. Instructor's name, office address, telephone number, and office hours.

4. Year and name of term or semester the course is being offered, and, possibly, class meeting times.

5. Some instructors head their course outlines with quotations to set the mood or theme of the course. Sonoma State College Library used the following for a course entitled Applied Library Research: "Every investigator must begin with a bibliography and end with a better bibliography."—George Sarton.

6. Texts and/or selected readings should be listed in a proper bibliographic format.

7. A general statement of the course objectives or purpose should be provided. This can be the same statement of purpose that was described in the "Designing the Course" section of this chapter. An extremely detailed outline might include the objectives for each unit of the course.

8. Course requirements should be spelled out.

9. A statement on grading policy or method of evaluation is wise. Some instructors list the number of points that will be granted for each assignment, while others specify the percentage of the total grade the various activities will comprise. Items eight and nine are often combined into one unit; for example, the following was taken from a course outline from the Lynchburg College Library:

> COURSE REQUIREMENTS: (Each counts as one-third of the final grade)
>
> 1. *Class assignments*
>   Each assignment will consist of 100 points. Extra credit may be earned by completing more than the required number assigned. Ten points will be de-

ducted for assignments turned in late. Weekly assignments are due on the Monday or Tuesday before the next class period.

2. *Subject bibliography*
   Compile a selective term bibliography on a subject chosen by the student and approved by the instructors. See the bibliography instruction sheet for more detailed information.
3. *Final exam*
   Specifics to be given later.

10. The course outline itself may be specific as to dates and assignments, or may simply list the order in which certain topics will be covered. A fairly specific outline might read:

December 15	Bibliographies DECLARE TERM BIBLIOGRAPHY PROJECT Read: Gates, Ch. 13 Turabian, Ch. 1 & 2

whereas a more general one might simply indicate:

Session 2	History of Books and Libraries

Most course outlines include dates of major examinations, if such have been scheduled, and dates when projects or major assignments are due. This helps the students plan their schedules.

TEACHING METHODS

The discussion which follows touches briefly on some standard teaching techniques as they apply to instruction in library use. A few basic books on teaching methods, aimed primarily at the college teacher, are listed at the end of the chapter and provide a starting point for further study of such complex topics as lecture and discussion methods and testing.

Reading Assignments

If reading assignments are to be included in the course requirements, select a textbook or have articles or books placed on reserve. Assistance in interpreting copyright laws may be available from the librarian in charge of reserves or interlibrary loan, or by consulting with teaching faculty in other departments to find out what procedures are currently being followed. A reading assignment is often used to prepare the student for a class discussion or exercise, or it may be used to reinforce what the student has learned in class and through exercises. It can also give the student something to refer to, to study for review, and to consult if he or she has failed to understand certain information presented in class.

Reading assignments also give the students an opportunity to work on their own, and often provide a different version of information presented in class. Some students learn better by reading, others by lecture or discussion; therefore, several approaches to the same topic can be helpful.

The reading assignments should be clearly related to the goals and objectives of particular units of the course. It is often difficult, if not impossible, to find a text or collection of articles which exactly meets this need. In time, many teachers develop their own texts or collections of readings for their courses. Many assign one basic text in a sequence that suits their syllabus, and supplement it with reserve readings or handouts on particular topics they wish to emphasize. Sometimes it is better to provide a lecture based on the teacher's reading, rather than require the students to read the same material.

Sometimes the reading assignment can be conveniently tied to a lesson on a particular reference tool. For example, students can be assigned to read the article on the library college in the *Encyclopedia of Education* as a means of both introducing them to that tool and preparing them for a discussion on the library-college concept.

The instructor will have to determine how much reading will be required of the students and how they will be held accountable for it. He or she might also want to consider incorporating a technique of assigning each student a particular topic to research, and have that student report back to the group. In this way practice in the techniques of independent research can be combined with learning about a particular subject. Care should be taken, however, that the entire course does not become simply a succession of student reports.

Lecture

A certain amount of lecturing is inevitable, and although the technique is less fashionable today than many others, it can be effective. Most people probably remember teachers who held them spellbound and caused ideas to race through their heads, using their skill as lecturers. It is important that the teacher believe in and convey the importance of the topic to the students. It is also important that the lecture be well organized and as carefully planned as a speech. It must be based on the goals and objectives of the course or unit. If the students are not understanding the material, it may be that the objectives are not completely clear. Examine them carefully.

Beware of trying to cover too much. Emphasize the search patterns that evolve in doing library research. Don't spend too much time on specific titles; rather, concentrate on formats of reference materials, how they are used, and how to find them. This will help students apply what they have learned through practical experience.

When lecturing, try to maintain eye contact and learn to judge the students' responses. If they show an interest, elucidate. Are they sleepy or yawning? Change the pace, interject questions, or try another approach to get their attention.

Find out what is of interest to the students. Provide examples which relate to everyday life. An explanation of Cutter numbers might include the fact that knowing how they are constructed can be helpful if you have neglected to write down a complete call number, or if you have written down a series of numbers but can no longer remember which number belonged to which book. It is often good to ask the students if they can think of any reasons why knowing a certain bit of information can be helpful.

Discussion

Lecturing is often effectively combined with discussion. There are teachers who can walk into a classroom, begin lecturing, and within five minutes have inspired an eager discussion. Yet it is often difficult to get discussion going. When students come into a classroom, it sometimes takes a while for their minds to turn from other things. As an opening gambit, "What did you read for today?" is likely to be greeted by blank looks and frantically searching minds, whereas a summary of what they have done in the previous session, thus leading into the assignment or topic for the day, will bring them to the subject.

Or begin with questions related to them, but indirectly related to the assignment. This technique is often used in course-related sessions, when one may well begin by asking how many have never been in the library before, how many have been in the stacks, what year or major they are, and how many have used the *Readers' Guide.* Skillful handling of discussion takes practice. For some people it is a natural talent, and others must work harder to be good at it.

The "discovery method" has been popular in recent years. This is basically the traditional Socratic method of leading students to "discover" a concept by asking them the right questions. The teacher avoids giving answers, and responds to questions with still more questions. It is a difficult technique to use well, but can be extremely effective. It is a technique which can sometimes be employed with interesting results in one-to-one instruction at the reference desk, and indeed may be considered an extension of the reference interview. It is often more effective to ask students when helping them with a citation in an index, for example, "What is the title of the article? Who is the author? On what pages will you find it?" and let them tell you, rather than to swiftly and efficiently point out the answers to them. Ask them if they can think of any other way they might find the information, gradually leading them to discover the keys, lists of abbreviations, and other information in the front of the volume. Such a technique fosters inquiring minds, self-reliance, and creative thinking on the part of the students—all qualities necessary for successful use of libraries. Somewhat easier to handle, and sometimes efficient than the strict discovery method is the more traditional lecture-discussion technique, where the teacher provides some information, but elicits response by asking questions.

A distinction is frequently made between closed and open-ended questions. The closed question seeks a specific piece of information: "Where would you look to find how many books by Ernest Hemingway are in this library?" The open-ended question asks: "How might you go about finding a list of Hemingway's books, and whether this library owns them or not?" In the first, we are looking for a specific answer: the card catalog. In the second, there is a wide range of acceptable answers, among them: *National Union Catalog,* Hemingway bibliographies, *Oxford Companion to American Literature,* and encyclopedia articles.

There is also the hypothetical, what-if type of question which can be invaluable in stimulating creative thinking. What if you had to select ten books to take along to a homestead in Alaska? on a solo sail around the world? to give to a college-bound high-school senior? to form the essential personal library for a person majoring in your subject area? Or: What are advantages and disadvantages of arranging the books in a library by size, color, author, title, subject?

When using discussion in the classroom it is frequently good to repeat the answer given by a student to make sure everyone has understood it. It is also helpful to stimulate students' comments and responses to each others' statements without intervention from the teacher. Give the students a chance to talk. It has been shown that even in the most participatory classes, the teacher does more talking than anyone else.

It can be helpful to sit in on classes taught by others, especially those of people with personalities and approaches similar to your own, to get ideas. Have someone observe your teaching and make suggestions or videotape your teaching sessions and later critique them.

Exercises, In and Out of Class

The hands-on experience provided by practical exercises is essential in teaching any skill. Students often think they understand until faced with the actual mechanics of a project. Nearly every available description of successful credit instruction stresses the importance of exercises, whether at the freshman, introductory, or graduate and professional level. Lecture, reading, and discussion can certainly prepare the student to analyze and use a particular reference work, but chances are, unless that person actually is required to pick up the book and use it for its intended purpose, he or she will soon forget what was "learned."

It is sometimes helpful to give students books to plunge into without any preparatory explanation. Lectures on the niceties of particular reference works can be deadly. On the other hand, a student's own discovery of the fine points of a particular work, and his communication of that discovery to his classmates, can be exciting and meaningful to all of them.

Care should be taken to design exercises that are interesting and meaningful. They should not be "busy work." Exercises requiring arranging book in call number order or having a fine knowledge of filing rules or corporate entries might better be bypassed in favor of exercises a step beyond these which require actual use of these skills. Yet care must be taken that the fundamentals are understood; otherwise the student, instructed in some of the finer points of the Library of Congress subject headings, may nevertheless look for his subject in the author-title section of the catalog or fail to discover that the *Journal of the American Medical Association* is in the periodicals listing after all—under the name of the association.

The exercises should also be designed with the goals and objectives of the course in mind. Many sample exercises are included in the texts listed at the end of the chapter. Others are available upon request from the various clearinghouses.

Workbooks

Workbooks, which were discussed in more detail in Chapter Five, can also be used as a teaching technique for credit courses, either alone or in conjunction with other methods.

Projects

Many credit courses include an extensive bibliographic project which requires the student to use the skills learned in the course. Such a project necessitates more sustained and coordinated effort than routine exercises, which are often useful preparation.

A typical bibliographic project requires the student to conduct a thorough search on a topic of his or her choice, and could be either one in which he or she has a personal interest or one which will be used to fulfill the requirements of another course. Some bibliographic projects are based on the "pathfinder" concept, in which an outline of a search strategy, including proper subject headings, is provided; while others are designed to follow a more traditional format such as a bibliographic essay.

When a bibliographic essay is required, the students must describe how they organized their search and what particular tools they used. Many bibliographic projects include annotations, which necessitates that the student be trained in methods of evaluating material. Others simply require that the student list a certain number of sources and also indicate how or where these sources were located. Most project descriptions remind the student that it is not the total number of citations that determines the value of the bibliography, but the variety and excellence of the sources that are chosen.

Another method of assigning the bibliographic project is to require two smaller projects. This allows for critiquing of the first in time to avoid the same errors in the second. A drawback to this method is that the students' efforts are split into two less substantial projects. In addition, it is difficult to fit two projects into the space of a term, especially if the first few lessons are necessary for learning background before the work can begin.

It is helpful to require from students a statement of their topic before they begin work on it, and to discuss with each student individually sources he or she might consult and methods that person might wish to use. Students often need help narrowing and focusing their project, but the project should not be so esoteric that the library does not have information on it.

If the project is also being used for another course, encourage the student to consult with that instructor also. The two instructors may wish to consult each other on evaluating the project. When the student's bibliographic project is used in conjunction with a term-paper project, it further emphasizes the practical application of library instruction, and will reinforce the student's learning and retention.

The following is a brief description of the bibliographic project assignment from the bibliographic project in the Applied Library Research course at Sonoma State College Library:

PROJECT—Requirement for 3 units

An annotated bibliography on a limited topic of approximately 25 items accompanied by a description of your search

> strategy. The entire project should be from 6 to 12 pages in length.
>
> We suggest that you pick a topic in which you have personal interest or one that ties directly to a research paper required by another instructor.
>
> Ideally your bibliography will not be simply a list of books, but a guide to the literature of the subject.
>
> Your project should be discussed with one of the instructors as early in the term as possible. By settling on a topic early the weekly assignment will become more meaningful. Try to use the library self-consciously, perhaps even keeping a diary of your methods, techniques, false starts, dead ends, discoveries, etc. as a preparation for your report on your search strategy.

Many bibliographic project descriptions are extremely detailed and lengthy. Most stipulate the bibliographic style form to be followed, emphasize the variety and types of materials to be included, and outline proper procedures for searching, notetaking, and evaluating.

Copies of a wide variety of bibliographic project outlines are available from the various clearinghouses. Many of the most useful for someone attempting to design a similar assignment are the most lengthy ones, which precludes reprinting them here.

Student Presentations

A desirable close to the course can be the students' oral presentations of their projects to the class. This allows the entire group to benefit from the work each has done. The knowledge that their work will be shared with someone other than the teacher may inspire the students to do a better job. Many students select a few outstanding items—books, audiovisual materials, maps, or the like—to show the class as a part of their presentation. It can be a refreshing change for both students and teacher to let the students do the teaching. If the class is so large that these presentations would take a disproportionate amount of time, they should either be very tightly scheduled or be avoided.

Audiovisual Aids

Audiovisual aids can provide variety and interest if they are well made and in keeping with the course's goals and objectives. It is difficult to find good, professionally packaged library films or slide-tape programs that are suitable for college-level students. The library may already have orientation tours or point-of-use packages which can be used. Don't neglect the blackboard, opaque and transparency projectors, posters, hand-made diagrams, flow-charts, and outlines. More detailed information on such AV materials is included in Chapter Eight.

Guest Speakers

Carefully chosen guest speakers can be an asset. They add variety to the class, and often provide a perspective and depth that the regular teacher cannot hope to match. But care must be taken that the speaker understands the nature of the class and what kind of presentation will be useful. It is often difficult to tell in advance who will make an effective, interesting guest speaker. Guest speakers must not be overused or the class will lack continuity and become a "lecture series" rather than a well-coordinated course. It is often good to lead a review discussion of a guest speakers' presentation, both to reinforce points that need emphasis and to evaluate the students' reactions to the speaker.

Tours or Field Trips

The same cautions that apply to guest speakers also apply to tours and field trips. They can be interesting, worthwhile, and provide new perspectives, but they can also be time-consuming and unrelated to the goals and objectives of the course. They should be carefully planned, and students should know in advance what they are expected to learn from them. If the trips last longer than the scheduled class period, many students may have difficulty attending. Such trips must be scheduled with care and discussed at the beginning of the course.

Tests

Tests should be learning experiences. They can also help evaluate the teacher's success and the students' progress. It is often helpful to pretest the students at the beginning of a course in order to find out how much they know already. This can also provide a base with which to compare the results of the posttests. It is also possible to rely totally on exercises and class projects for evaluation, rather than on tests. But many teachers find that tests stimulate learning and increase students' motivation. These may be unannounced pop quizzes or scheduled examinations. Whatever kinds of tests are used, they should, like every other aspect of the course, be based on its goals and objectives.

FORMAL AND INFORMAL EVALUATION

Many colleges and universities have standard student evaluation forms which can be used or are required to be used to evaluate all formal courses. These can often be useful. However, more evaluation is helpful, especially when one is offering a new course or teaching for the first time. There are ways of evaluating the course as a whole. It is possible to test students who have completed the course, and a control group. There is, again, a vast body of literature on formal evaluation of both teachers and courses. The books and articles listed at the end of this chapter provide a starting place for delving into this literature.

Informal evaluation is sometimes done almost unconsciously. Most speakers watch other people as they talk in order to evaluate their reactions to what is said, and adjust their responses accordingly. The same thing happens in the classroom. Most teachers have probably experienced the frustration of having a dozing student in one corner of the room, an intent, alert, eager beaver in the front hanging on every word, and a wide range of attitudes in between. It is usually to the middle group that the teacher plays.

In teaching a course for the first time, gauging student reaction carefully is very important. It is wise to be flexible enough to change strategies to those which work best, and to try a variety of methods and informally evaluate the success of each. Are students falling asleep during a lecture? Change emphasis, move on to a discussion group, or give them exercises instead. Are they bored with the exercises? Ask them what they see as the course's problems. Their responses can be helpful in determining what teaching methods will be most effective.

One important fact to remember is that the same techniques do not work for everyone. Students are different and teachers are different. Eventually every teacher builds up a personal repertoire of techniques that work. It is often surprising which methods students prefer. Sometimes the most carefully planned approaches fall flat, while a last-minute idea or improvisation, or some exercise decided on as uninteresting but necessary, turns out to be great. Be open, flexible, and prepared for any response.

Students sense a teacher's responsiveness, which in turn encourages their openness and receptivity. Nothing is worse than asking for their opinions and then ignoring them. Their advice needn't always be followed—sometimes the teacher is right—but let them know they have been heard and that their opinions have been considered.

PROMOTING THE COURSE

A new course will require publicity, especially if it is unique and does not fit into an established sequence of courses or into the program of a particular department. There is little agreement on the most effective way to publicize a new course. There are always the traditional direct methods such as posters, newspaper ads (which tend to be expensive), and handouts or flyers. It is also possible to announce library courses to tour groups.

A more effective way often is to work directly through other faculty members, departments, and advisors. If some of these people were helpful in getting the course established, a good start has been made. First-hand, person-to-person contact is important. Memos sent to advisors or faculty members announcing the course tend to be lost in piles of similar announcements unless a faculty member is personally interested in the course.

If the course is being offered through another department, or at the urging of a particular department, consider discussing the course and the rationale behind it at a faculty meeting. A demonstration of some sample lessons from the course can work wonders (many faculty members may realize they don't know much about the library themselves).

If the course is a general introductory library-skills course, consider compiling a list of courses which routinely require research papers. Most departments have files of course outlines which they are willing to share. Then professors of these courses can be contacted. If the library already has a course-related instruction program, contact the teachers who regularly make use of this program. They are already likely to be convinced of the necessity for library instruction and they may be willing to recommend the course to their students (as either teachers or advisors) and to fellow faculty members. It may be possible to meet with some of these course-related instruction supporters as a group, to explain the course to them and elicit their help.

If the course can achieve standing as part of the requirements for a degree, or as a recommended option for fulfillment of specified requirements, this will help. In fact, it may make a great difference in the projected size of enrollment.

Whether or not the course is required, scheduling is extremely important. Students must be able to fit such "elected" or "required" courses into their schedules. If possible, conflicts with required courses or labs should be avoided. Various time slots should be tried until one seems better than the rest. If the enrollment is large enough, it may be possible to offer a morning and an afternoon session.

Difficulty in promoting the course may be directly related to the size of the institution and the closeness of ties already existing between librarians and the teaching faculty. It may be possible for the course initiator or instructor, the library director, or a library representative to a body such as a faculty senate or college faculty group, to present information about the course to this group, urging its support. In days of increasing lamentation about the poor quality of students' basic skills, a library-skills course can offer a ray of hope to discouraged faculty members. Testimony by some of the teaching faculty on behalf of the course, evidence from them that library instruction has significantly improved the quality of their students' work, may be the most helpful kind of support. If library instruction is new to the institution, testimony gathered from the literature concerning results at other institutions can be helpful. Once the course is under way, it becomes its own best advertisement. As word about the usefulness of the course spreads among the students, attendance should grow.

Nevertheless, the necessity of support from the teaching faculty cannot be overemphasized. A successful separate course cannot exist in a vacuum. If faculty members are no longer requiring research papers and library work of their students, there will be no motivation and no need for library-skills courses. The faculty may no longer be requiring library work because it has become discouraged by the poor quality of work its students have produced. Thus there is a vicious cycle of poor-quality work, discouragement, and defeat on the part of the faculty, resulting in lowered standards and poorer education for the students.

If librarians are going to convince the teaching faculty that library-skills teaching can make a difference, they are going to have to believe this themselves, be extremely well prepared, and able to convince faculty members that librarians have something valuable to offer, not only to the students, but to them. Again, the closer the existing working relationship is and the more respect the teaching faculty already has for librarians, the easier the job will be.

It is in the face of this overwhelming need to promote library instruction that many librarians rebel. It takes a tremendous amount of time, and it means putting oneself on the line and selling oneself. As it is, many librarians find teaching a difficult task to take on. Unlike the teacher's role, which traditionally requires a touch of missionary zeal and self-promotion, the librarian's role tends to encourage unassuming, retiring, and reactive behavior. The teacher has traditionally had to stand up and say, "O.K., everybody, look at me and pay attention to what I have to say!" whereas the librarian politely waits to be asked for help or perhaps discreetly volunteers assistance to the lost and confused.

Nevertheless, to establish a new program to broaden the scope of traditional academic concerns, it is necessary to be a bit of a missionary. Read the arguments in favor of library instruction again; reread Daniel Gore, whose enthusiasm is contagious. Gain the support first of all of the more dynamic members of the library administration. They may be able to pave the way to communicate with the teaching faculty. Consult the chapter on program planning. Analyze the situation, then tackle the problems, and plan the course in the way that seems best.

FOOTNOTES

1. John M. Tucker, "The Origins of Bibliographic Instruction in Academic Libraries, 1876-1914," *New Horizons for Academic Libraries, ACRL 1978 National Conference-Contributed Papers* (Chicago: American Library Association, 1978).
2. Daniel Gore, "Anachronistic Wizard: The College Reference Librarian," *Library Journal* 89:1,690 (15 April 1964).
3. Ibid., p. 1,690.
4. James Kennedy, "Question: A Separate Course in Bibliography or Course-related Instruction?" in Sul H. Lee, ed., *Conference on Library Orientation, 1st, Eastern Michigan Univer-*

sity, 1971, Library Orientation Papers (Ann Arbor: Pierian, 1972), pp. 18-28.

5. John A. Bollier, "Bibliographic Instruction in the Graduate/ Professional Theological School," *New Horizons for Academic Libraries, ACRL 1978 National Conference-Contributed Papers* (Chicago: American Library Association, 1978).
6. Ibid., p. 10.
7. Ibid.
8. Anne Roberts, *A Study of Ten SUNY Campuses Offering an Undergraduate Credit Course in Library Instruction* (Arlington, Va.: ERIC Document Reproduction Service, ED 157 529, 1978) 81 pp.
9. Gore, p. 1,691.
10. Howard W. Dillon, "Organizing the Academic Library for Instruction," *Journal of Academic Librarianship* 1:4-7 (September 1975).
11. Gore, p. 1,690.

SUGGESTED READINGS

The Credit Course in Bibliography

Blum, Mark E. and Spangehl, Stephen. *Introducing the College Student to Academic Inquiry: An Individualized Course in Library Research Skills.* ERIC Educational Document Reproduction Service, 1977. ED 152 315. 35 pp.

Bollier, John. "Bibliographic Instruction in the Graduate/ Professional Theological School," in *New Horizons for Academic Libraries, ACRL 1978 National Conference-Contributed Papers.* Chicago: American Library Association, 1978.

Eyman, David H. and Nunley, Alven C., Jr. *The Effectiveness of Library Science 1011 in Teaching Bibliographic Skills.* ERIC Educational Document Reproduction Service, 1978. ED 150 962. 30 pp.

Gore, Daniel. "A Course in Bibliography for Freshmen at Asheville-Biltmore College." *North Carolina Libraries* 23 (1965):80.

Gore, Daniel. "Anachronistic Wizard: The College Reference Librarian." *Library Journal* 89 (April 15, 1964):1,688-1,692.

Kennedy, James. "Question: A Separate Course in Bibliography or Course-Related Library Instruction?" in Sul H. Lee, ed., *Conference on Library Orientation, 1st, Eastern Michigan University, 1971, Library Orientation Papers,* pp. 18-28. Ann Arbor: Pierian, 1972.

Kirkendall, Carolyn, ed. "Library Instruction: A Column of Opinion." *Journal of Academic Librarianship* 3 (March 1977): 94-95.

LaRose, Al and Young, Barbara. "A Librarian in the Classroom," in Barbara Mertins, comp., *Bibliographic Instruction,* pp. 12-19. West Virginia Library Association. Working Conference of the College and University Section. ERIC Educational Document Reproduction Service, 1977. ED 144 582.

Peterschmidt, Mary Jo. "Experiences: Team Teaching Library Instruction at San Jose State College." *Instruction in the Use of the College and University Library.* Selected Conference Papers, July 13-14, 1970 Conference Workshop, University of California at Berkeley. ERIC Educational Document Reproduction Service, 1970. ED 045 103.

Rader, Hannelore B. "Formal Courses in Bibliography," in John Lubans, Jr., ed., *Educating the Library User,* pp. 279-285. New York: Bowker, 1975.

Rettig, James. *General Library Skills Courses Offered for Credit* 1977. (25 page paper avail. from Project LOEX, Eastern Michigan University, Center of Educational Resources, Ypsilanti, MI 48197.)

Roberts, Anne. *A Study of Ten SUNY Campuses Offering an Undergraduate Credit Course in Library Instruction.* ERIC Educational Document Reproduction Service, 1978. ED 157 529. 81 pp.

Shain, Charles. "Bibliography I: The U.C. Berkeley Experience." *Instruction in the Use of the College and University Library.* Selected Conference Papers, July 13-14, 1970 Conference Workshop, University of California at Berkeley. ERIC Educational Document Reproduction Service, 1970. ED 045 103.

Walser, Katina P. and Kruse, Kathryn W. "A College Course for Nurses on the Utilization of Library Resources." *Bulletin of the Medical Library Association* 65 (April 1977):265-267.

Weir, Katherine M. "The Teaching Library." *Special Libraries Association. Geography and Map Division Bulletin.* September 1977, pp. 34-39.

Teaching Methods

Davis, James R. *Teaching Strategies for the College Classroom.* Boulder, Colo.: Westview (Westview Special Studies in Higher Education), 1976.

Heim, Alice. *Teaching and Learning in Higher Education.* Windsor, Berks, England: NFER Publishing Co., 1976.

McKeachie, Wilbert J. *Teaching Tips: A Guidebook for the Beginning College Teacher.* 7th ed. Lexington, Mass.: D.C. Heath, 1978.

Nuthall, Graham and Snook, Ivan. "Contemporary Models of Teaching," in Robert M. W. Travers, ed., *Second Handbook of Research on Teaching,* pp. 47-76. Chicago: Rand McNally, 1973.

Revill, D. H. "Teaching Methods in the Library: A Survey from an Educational Point of View." *Library World* 71 (February 1970):243-248.

Selected Texts for Introductory Courses

Cook, Margaret. *The New Library Key.* 3rd ed. New York: Wilson, 1975.

Downs, Robert B. and Keller, Clara O. *How to Do Library Research.* 2nd ed. Urbana: Univ. of Illinois Pr., 1975.

Gates, Jean K. *Guide to the Use of Books and Libraries.* 4th ed. New York: McGraw-Hill, 1979.

Gore, Daniel. *Bibliography for Beginners.* 2nd ed. New York: Appleton, 1973.

Hauer, Mary G. et al. *Books, Libraries and Research.* Dubuque, Ia.: Kendall/Hunt, 1979.

Katz, William. *Your Library: A Reference Guide.* New York: Holt, 1979.

Lolley, John L. *Your Library—What's in It for You?* New York: Wiley, 1974.

CHAPTER 7

Computer-Assisted Instruction

INTRODUCTION

Computer-assisted instruction (CAI) in academic libraries reached its zenith in the early 1970s, when ample funds were available for experimentation. Ironically, as libraries have increasingly turned to automated circulation systems, card catalogs, and bibliographic databases, and as computer terminals have become commonplace in libraries, the use of CAI for teaching library skills has virtually disappeared.

Indicative of the changing role of CAI in libraries is the fact that Lubans' 1974 *Educating the Library User* devotes an entire chapter to the topic, while his 1978 *Progress in Educating the Library User* contains but one brief paragraph pronouncing:

> Computer-assisted instruction (CAI) is still only of peripheral interest in library instruction programs. It has little application for educating large numbers of users since the terminals and software are extremely expensive. Perhaps as libraries become more automated and the cost of equipment drops, CAI may eventually find a place in programs of educating library users.[1]

A survey of recent literature on CAI indicates that although there has been some decline from the initial enthusiasm of the sixties and early seventies, CAI is alive and well in such areas as medicine, the sciences, business, and economics. It may be that CAI lends itself more readily to the structure of the sciences, or that the professionals in those fields are more comfortable with the structure and technology of the computer than public-service librarians. Whatever the explanation, it is to these fields that librarians must turn for information on the latest developments in CAI.

The two most significant library CAI programs in the literature are Marina Axeen's experimental use of CAI to teach an introductory library-skills course at the University of Illinois in the late 1960s[2] and Patricia Culkin's work at the University of Denver.[3] Although both programs were judged successful, only the University of Denver's program has continued through the 1970s. Other libraries have experimented with CAI from time to time, but there is little information available about their programs.[4]

Denver's program nicely illustrates two patterns of CAI applications in libraries. The first is the "traditional" use of CAI to teach library skills. This is also the type of program Axeen used at Illinois, although her program was organized as a credit course while Denver's is designed as point-of-use instruction. The second, which holds exciting potential for the online library, is a CAI program with the capability of being linked directly to a bibliographic database.

Denver's "traditional" CAI program teaches students how to use periodical indexes, abstracting services, and the card catalog, and how to research a term paper. Its newer program, called a "query analysis system," allows the students to work through a search on a topic of their choice, and presents the possibility of tying in with established bibliographic databases. For example, the students learn through the query analysis program which subject headings are appropriate for searching a particular topic in various indexes. By the time they have completed the program, they will have more clearly defined their topic and will know that they can find information on it in the *Social Sciences Index*, for example, under certain subject headings, and in *Sociological Abstracts* under others.

At present the Denver program is not linked to a commercial search, but further development of the query analysis system presents the possibility of eventually training the user to do his or her own online searching. One such program already in existence is Medlearn, developed at the National Library of Medicine and available through the Medlars system.[5] The program has been enthusiastically received by Medline users (librarians, library-school students, medical professionals, and others), and there are plans for its expansion.[6]

Another self-training system has been developed by DIALOG. The purpose of this database, called ONTAP,[7] is to provide practice exercises for searchers trying to become proficient in the DIALOG System. Both ONTAP and Medlearn have been developed to instruct the users of a particular system. With in-house computer systems, similar programming could be planned and developed. Practice programs would then be available for training both professional and nonprofessional library personnel on the in-house system.

In addition to the potential use of CAI for in-house training, there is the recent explosion of online bibliographic databases to consider. As far removed as it seems, it may not be too far in the future that patrons will begin to do their own searching. Already there are some databases that do not have comparable printed indexes. Some libraries have even canceled expensive, minimally used printed abstracts and indexes, and in return offer free searches of the online version. Eventually libraries may not be able to cope with the number of searches that are requested, and training patrons to do their own searching will be a necessity. Since the equipment is available, CAI may be the most effective mode to accomplish this.

Aside from this idea of self-training for bibliographic database searching, there is even more immediate application for CAI. For those libraries planning online catalogs, there will be a need for some type of user instruction. Again, since the equipment is available, CAI becomes a logical as well as convenient choice. This is hardly a unique or innovative concept. In fact, some large computer corporations now rely on online training for users of their programs. According to Walter J. Doherty of the IBM Watson Research Laboratory, "The text which tells a person how to use a program should be contained in the program itself and it is our common practice to do this . . . Because on-line documentation is available in my daily use of computers at Yorktown, I have not had to open our IBM Manual for the past few years."[8]

It should be noted, however, that it is a difficult if not impossible task to superimpose instructional text on programs that have already been developed. Two Ohio librarians who have struggled to design programs for training their Library Control System users advise, "First of all, begin at the beginning: start planning for public use of any computer system right along with the initial program itself."[9] Because opportunities were missed at the beginning of the development of the online access system at Ohio State, these librarians are not certain that a tutorial program on the same terminal as the database will ever be possible. "The problems here of hardware and hookups have held us back and may prove to be insurmountable."[10]

Since many libraries are not as far along with online systems as Ohio State, it is possible for them to "begin at the beginning." There should be close communication between those planning automated systems and those responsible for user education. Since the computer is at the heart of any online library, its capability to instruct should not be ignored. Computer-assisted instruction is returning to the library and some day it may be as common as the opening of a card-catalog drawer.

PROS AND CONS OF CAI

There has never been any research which conclusively demonstrates the superiority of one method of instruction (including computer-assisted instruction) over another.

Marina Axeen found, in a comparison of her CAI and traditional lecture-discussion groups, no significant difference in test scores.[11] This result agreed with previous studies. More recently, a 1978 summary of research continues to support this evidence: "Published studies comparing the effectiveness of CAI to traditional instruction report conflicting results, but generally conclude that CAI is at least as effective (55 percent) and often more effective (45 percent)."[12]

Advantages of Computer-Assisted Instruction

There are, however, some distinct advantages to using CAI, which have been noted by various researchers. These may be divided into benefits to the student, to the teacher, and to the institution.

Some of the advantages to the student are:

1. The versatility and flexibility of most CAI programs make the learning more interesting than printed programmed texts.
2. Students can proceed at their own pace and enter that program at any level they choose.
3. The student gets immediate feedback from the computer, a factor which has been shown to increase learning.
4. The student can learn the same amount in less time than through lecture-discussion.[13]
5. In the case of an online tutorial system such as Medlearn, the student uses the same format and syntax as the system he or she is learning, and "therefore, almost unconsciously, the Medlearn student becomes familiar and comfortable with the conventions of communicating with Medline."[14]

Among advantages to the teacher are:

1. The program can free the teacher from basic instruction, allowing more time to deal with complex problems.

2. The program is easy to revise once it has been set up. There is no need to change multiple copies, or review and revise lecture notes before each class.
3. A complete record of students' progress can be kept by the computer, eliminating the need for time-consuming testing and grading of tests.
4. CAI can impose sound instructional techniques on the teacher, a fact which can be especially helpful to librarians because so few of them have had training in educational techniques.

Some advantages to the institution are:

1. Although the initial cost of setting up the program is high, once this has been done, personnel costs can be reduced.
2. A CAI program can be used in widely scattered geographical locations.
3. The program can keep its own records and evaluate itself.
4. Slavens, in his 1969 article on the use of CAI in teaching reference librarians in library schools, points out four problems in library-school instruction which CAI can help remedy. These are equally applicable to most library-use instruction programs:
   (1) shortage of faculty members
   (2) inadequate teaching methods
   (3) widely varying background of students
   (4) lack of self-instructional materials (they quickly become outdated as new reference materials are published).[15]

Disadvantages of Computer-Assisted Instruction

Most of the disadvantages of CAI have already been mentioned in passing. They include the following:

1. The initial development of the program is very costly. Administrators are reluctant to gamble vast quantities

of funds on a technique they are not convinced is going to work. The current unpopularity of CAI in libraries and current tightness of funds makes this reluctance even more difficult to overcome.

2. There is a need for machinery (terminals) and access to a computer. As libraries rely more and more on computers and as the cost of equipment decreases, this disadvantage may disappear. The advent of mini- and micro-computers may also help cut costs and down time.
3. CAI terminals are stationary. The student cannot move around with them from one part of the library to another to complete exercises requiring the use of library materials, as can currently be done with a programmed textbook. Again, as terminals become smaller and more portable, and as libraries turn to online reference materials, this disadvantage will disappear.
4. As the use of computerized databases continues to grow, and the vendors of these databases begin to design their systems for the primary user rather than the librarian, they will undoubtedly also design tutorial sequences into their programs, just as every Wilson index now has a "How to Use" section in each volume. Therefore, time spent by libraries now on CAI systems may result in systems that will soon be outmoded, while new systems will be available through commercial vendors at lower costs.

Summary

These disadvantages should not necessarily outweigh the advantages of CAI. There is still room for exploration and experimentation. It may be a grave mistake to relinquish all development of CAI to commercial vendors if libraries are going to retain their role as providers of free access to information.

STEPS FOR PLANNING A CAI PROGRAM

1. Do as much background reading as possible on CAI. Look to other skill disciplines that are somewhat parallel to the teaching of library skills.

2. Decide upon the library skills that could be used with CAI. Will the CAI programs constitute complete courses or will the programs be selective? How will this library instruction activity fit into the curriculum? Will it be a required or elective course? How many students can the program handle? Where will the hardware be located? Will extra personnel be needed?

3. Look for opportunities that may be in existence on campus. There may be a CAI laboratory that is open to all departments. There may be a computer that could be used via telephone hookup. The library may have an automated system that could be adapted for the purpose of CAI. It is essential to talk with resource persons who can provide information, both about programming and cost.

4. Contact vendors and discover what they may have to offer. There may be commercially packaged programs which can be adapted to particular pieces of equipment. It may be possible to use a telephone hookup to a vendor computer. Find out the cost and the estimated elapsed time between the signing of the contract and the availability of CAI to the user.

5. By this point, there should be a clear picture of what would be involved, and an estimated cost for the project. If CAI is still considered feasible, the rationale for such a program and the implementation plans should be written into some type of document. This should be presented to the library administration. Although the administration may have been aware of the preplanning, this formalized document outlines the proposed program and allows for administrative input.

6. The key to administrative acceptance of the CAI project may be funding. It is at this stage that sources of funding should be pursued. They may be from an outside source, or

there may be designated funds within the institution which can be requested. The library administrators may be willing to provide seed money or matching funds. It will be necessary to arrive at an estimated budget no matter how funding is approached.

7. When administrative approval is given and the finances are available, work can begin with the individuals who will be setting up the CAI program for the library. Establishing a CAI program is normally a team effort between a librarian, an educational technologist, and a programmer. The librarian outlines what is desired, and the technologist and programmer work to translate the material into machine language.

8. Order the necessary equipment. This may include terminal and telephone lines.

9. While working with the outside consultants, begin to develop any textual material that will accompany the units of the program. Also make arrangements for supplementary material such as catalog cards, periodical indexes, and so forth. It may be desirable to set up learning activities packages. Such packages may include samples of the material being discussed, exercise sheets, and possibly an assignment to be completed in the library.

10. When the programming is ready, there should be a pilot project to help work out the bugs. New staff members are a good group to use the first time through the program.

11. Working with the technologist and programmer, revise areas of the program presenting problems. The more times the program is used, the better the feedback. There should be a number of trial runs before any CAI is considered ready for use.

12. When the program, textual and supplementary materials are ready, classes, groups, or individuals may be scheduled. The many details about hardware access, hours available, advising time, scheduling, and so on, must be planned, and such information should be included in a handbook or policy manual.

13. Continual monitoring of programs and users is essential. Even the best of programs may need updates and re-

visions. Equipment should be checked for wear, and inoperative pieces should be repaired or replaced.

14. There should be a continual evaluation of the program. The programs can be written to include periodic reviews and tests. These provide immediate feedback to the user. Records of such tests can be stored for future evaluation by the instructors. Longitudinal studies can also be useful. The reaction of the CAI user is valuable, and may be measured before and after the user's involvement with the program.

FOOTNOTES

1. Betty L. Hacker and Joel S. Rutstein, "Educating Large Numbers of Users in University Libraries: An Analysis and a Case Study," in John Lubans, Jr., ed., *Progress in Educating the Library User* (New York: Bowker, 1978), p. 109.
2. Marina E. Axeen, *Teaching Library Use to Undergraduates-Comparison of Computer-based Instruction and the Conventional Lecture. Final Report* (Bethesda, Md.: ERIC Educational Document Reproduction Service, ED 014 316, 1968).
3. Four articles describing the Denver program are:
   Patricia B. Culkin, "CAI Experiment," *American Libraries* 3:643-645 (June 1972).
   ———, "Instructional Materials: Design and Development. Computer-assisted Instruction in Library Use," *Drexel Library Quarterly* 8:301-311 (July 1972).
   Lois N. Hansen, "Program Evaluation. Computer-assisted Instruction in Library Use: An Evaluation," *Drexel Library Quarterly* 8:345-355 (June 1972).
   Ward Shaw, Patricia B. Culkin, and Thomas E. Drabek, "The Query Analysis System: A Progress Report," *New Horizons for Academic Libraries. ACRL 1978 National Conference-Contributed Papers.* (Chicago: American Library Association, 1978), 19 pp.
4. Cynthia Aman, *A Survey of Computer-assisted Instruction in Academic Library Instruction* (1977). (Four page paper avail. from Project LOEX, Eastern Michigan University, Center of Educational Resources, Ypsilanti, MI 48197.)
5. Laura J. Eisenberg, et al., "Medlearn: A Computer-Assisted

(CAI) Program for MEDLARS," *Bulletin of the Medical Library Association* 66:6-13 (January 1978).

6. Telephone conversation with Laura Eisenberg (now Kasselbaum), Spring 1978.
7. "ONTAP: Online Training and Practice," *Cronolog: Monthly Newsletter of DIALOG Information Retrieval Service* 5:2 (January 1977).
8. Quoted in *Computation Center Bulletin,* The Pennsylvania State University, (January 16-31, 1979), p. 4.
9. Gail Herndon and Noelle Van Pulis, "The On-line Library: Problems and Prospects for User Education," *New Horizons for Academic Libraries. ACRL 1978 National Conference-Contributed Papers.* (Chicago: American Library Association, 1978), 19 pp.
10. Ibid., p. 9.
11. Axeen, p. 52.
12. Errol M. Magidson, "Issue Overview: Trends in Computer-assisted Instruction," *Educational Technology* 18:7 (April 1978).
13. Axeen, p. 11.
14. Eisenberg, p. 12.
15. Thomas P. Slavens, "Computer-assisted Instruction for Reference Librarians," *Journal of Education for Librarians* 4:116 (Fall 1969).

SUGGESTED READINGS

Computer-Assisted Instruction: Applications in Teaching Library Use

Aman, Cynthia. "*A Survey of Computer-assisted Instruction in Academic Library Instruction,*" 1977. (Unpublished four page paper avail. from Project LOEX, Eastern Michigan University, Center of Educational Resources, Ypsilanti, MI 48197.)

Axeen, Marina E. *Teaching Library Use to Undergraduates—Comparison of Computer-based Instruction and the Conventional Lecture. Final Report.* ERIC Educational Document Reproduction Service, 1968. ED 014 316.

Block, Karen R. "Computer-assisted Instruction," in *Encyclopedia of Library and Information Science,* Vol. 5, pp. 515-538. New York: Dekker, 1971.

Clark, Alice S. "Computer-assisted Instruction," in John Lubans, Jr., ed., *Educating the Library User,* pp. 336-349. New York: Bowker, 1974.

Culkin, Patricia B. "CAI Experiment." *American Libraries* 3 (June 1972):643-645.

Culkin, Patricia B. "Instructional Materials: Design and Development. Computer-assisted Instruction in Library Use." *Drexel Library Quarterly* 8 (July 1972): 301-311.

Eisenberg, Laura J., Standing, Roy A., Tidball, Charles S., and Leiter, Joseph. "Medlearn: A Computer-assisted (CAI) Program for MEDLARS." *Bulletin of the Medical Library Association* 66 (January 1978): 6-13.

Hansen, Lois N. "Program Evaluation—Computer-assisted Instruction in Library Use: An Evaluation." *Drexel Library Quarterly* 8 (July 1972): 345-355.

Herndon, Gail and Van Pulis, Noelle. "The On-line Library: Problems and Prospects for User Education." *New Horizons for Academic Libraries. ACRL 1978 National Conference—Contributed Papers.* Chicago: American Library Association, 1978. 19pp.

Lyon, Becky J. "Mind Transplants, or the Role of Computer-assisted Instruction in the Future of the Library," in F. W. Lancaster, ed., *The Use of Computers in Literature Searching and Related Reference Activities in Libraries.* Clinic on Library Applications of Data Processing, 1975. Urbana, Ill.: University of Illinois Pr., 1976.

McCoy, Ralph E. "Automation in Freshmen Library Instruction." *Wilson Library Bulletin* 36 (February 1962): 468-470.

Primus, W. J. and White, J. D. *On Line Techniques for Teaching in Library and Information Science: Final Report.* British Library Research and Development Report 5357. Loughborough, England: Loughborough University of Technology, Department of Library and Information Studies, 1977. 32 pp.

Shaw, Ward, Culkin, Patricia B., and Drabek, Thomas E. "The Query Analysis System: A Progress Report." *New Horizons for Academic Libraries. ACRL 1978 National Conference—Contributed Papers.* Chicago: American Library Association, 1978. 19 pp.

Show and Tell: A Clinic on Using Media in Library Instruction. Paper presented at the American Library Association Annual Conference 1972. ERIC Educational Document Reproduction Service, 1973. ED 067 841. 32 pp.

Slavens, Thomas P. "Computer-assisted Instruction for Reference Librarians." *Journal of Education for Librarians* 10 (Fall 1969): 116-119.

Selected Books and Articles on Computer-Assisted Instruction

Bagley, Carole A. "So You Want to Do CAI? First You Need to Select Hardware, Software, Courseware . . ." *National Society for Performance and Instruction: NSPI Journal* (March 1979): 35-36.

Dyer, Charles A. *Preparing for Computer-assisted Instruction.* Englewood Cliffs, N.J.: Educational Technology Publications, 1972.

Hunter, Beverly, et al. *Learning Alternatives in U.S. Education: Where Student and Computer Meet.* Englewood Cliffs, N.J.: Educational Technology Publications, 1975.

Leiblum, Mark. "A Pragmatic Approach to Initiating a Computer-assisted Instruction Service and Some Problems Involved." *Programmed Learning and Instructional Technology* 14 (August 1977): 243-249.

Magidson, Errol, ed. "Trends in CAI. Symposium." *Educational Technology* 18 (April 1978): 5-63.

Stolurow, Lawrence M. "Computer-aided Instruction," in *Encyclopedia of Education,* pp. 390-400.

Yngstrom, Louise. "A Method for Analysis and Construction of Interactive Computer-based Teaching Programmes," in O. Lecarme and R. Lewis, eds., *Computers in Education,* pp. 37-40. New York: North American Elsevier, 1975.

SOURCES OF ADDITIONAL INFORMATION

Association for the Development of Computer-based Instructional Systems (ADCIS). Computer Center, Western Washington State College, Bellingham, Wash. 98225. Purpose: to advance the investigation and utilization of CAI.

Educational Technology (magazine). Educational Technology Publications, 140 Sylvan Ave., Englewood Cliffs, NJ 07632.

ENTELEK, CAI/CMI Information Exchange, 42 Pleasant St., Newburyport, MA 01950.

Academic Computing Directory, 1977. Human Resources Research Organization, 300 N. Washington St., Alexandria, VA 22314.

Journal of Computer-based Instruction (quarterly). Association for the Development of Computer-based Instructional Systems, 3255 Hennepin Ave., S., Minneapolis, MN 55408.

National Society for Performance and Instruction: NSPI Journal. 1126 16th St. NW, Suite 313, Washington, DC 20036.

CHAPTER 8

Audiovisual Materials and Equipment

The use of audiovisual materials (AV) is quite appropriate in any library instruction program. In fact, librarians have been quite successful in adapting slides, filmstrips, videotapes, films, and transparencies to meet a variety of instructional needs. Many of these uses have been illustrated in previous chapters, but the specifics of audiovisual material and equipment need a more detailed examination.

In looking at the ways that librarians use the various types of AV, three functions can be distinguished. The most basic function that AV serves is that of support material for classroom instruction. Teachers find it advantageous to use the blackboard, overhead transparencies, or a slide program to supplement and illustrate the classroom lecture material. Credit courses, lectures, seminars, or course-related sessions could all be enhanced by the use of such media.

A second use of AV is for point-of-use instruction. This will often involve slide-tape or video programs that explain the process of using such materials as *Science Citation Index* or *Psychological Abstracts*. The programs can be used with a class, but they can also be made available for self-instruction.

In contrast to the limited scope of point-of-use programs

are the more general AV programs developed around themes, which may include "How to Use the Library for Research," "Orientation to the Library," "Using Government Documents," or "Reference Sources in Education." Such slide-tape or video shows cover a broad range of material and are designed to provide an overview of the topics rather than a close-up examination of one particular tool.

No matter what role AV is chosen to serve, there are certain basic requirements. First, there is a need for the appropriate equipment (or hardware). Secondly, the necessary software (e.g., transparencies, films, slides) must be purchased or developed. The third requirement is that of trained personnel to use both the hardware and software. With this in mind, the following is a discussion of the specifics involved in the use of audiovisual materials in a library's instructional program.

AUDIOVISUAL EQUIPMENT

One of the requirements mentioned for the use of AV is the appropriate equipment. Many libraries, particularly those that are tied in with a media center, have equipment readily available. Other libraries are able to use the general audiovisual services offered for the entire campus. Still other libraries find it necessary or desirable to purchase hardware for internal use. No matter what the means of access to the equipment, it is advisable that an instructional program have the following: a blackboard, an overhead projector, a slide projector, a cassette tape player that is compatible with the slide projector, a screen, and appropriate carts for the equipment. Less basic, but useful, are opaque projectors, filmstrip projectors, movie projectors, videotape units, flip charts, headsets, and sound/slide projectors with a built-in screen. Each of these items will be discussed briefly and some suggestions will be included for their use in a library instruction program.

The blackboard is truly an AV tool and has been for many

years. It is often permanently mounted on a classroom wall, but there are portable models. Blackboards provide a place for an instructor to write his or her name, office address, and telephone number. It also can be used for clarifying discussions. An outline of activities for a class session may be listed on the board or sample cards from the card catalog may be drawn for the purpose of illustration. In general, it is an excellent support tool for classroom lectures and seminars.

Not all libraries are equipped with classroom space and blackboards. For such libraries it may be beneficial to have a flip chart. This is a large tablet of paper that is set up on a stand that is somewhat similar to an artist's easel. Felt pens or crayons are most effective for visibility. As each sheet of paper is used, it can be flipped over the back of the stand. Flip charts can be used for the same purposes as blackboards.

The overhead projector is probably the most practical piece of AV hardware for classroom use. By using an overhead the instructor is able to show examples that everyone in the room can see. At the same time, the instructor has full control over the material being presented. Overheads are relatively inexpensive and are simple to operate. The overhead projects and enlarges transparencies, which are rolls or sheets of clear plastic. Transparencies can be drawn on with wax or grease pencils or felt pens. With such a technique the instructor can use transparencies for outlines, notes, illustrations, examples of subject headings, and the like. Besides the hand-drawn or handwritten ones, transparencies can also be made through a variety of processes.[1] The most convenient is photoduplicating. Transparencies can be made as quickly as paper copies with such machines. Other methods include a spirit-duplicator process and a diazo (ammonia) process.

Prepared transparencies can be used over and over. It is very easy to develop sets that reflect a theme or subject emphasis. If, for example, a music-education class comes in for a class lecture every term, it is efficient to have a transparency set that has samples from the card catalog, *LC Subject Headings, ERIC, Education Index,* and the serial holdings list that show a music-education theme. Such sets can be put together for almost any class that is being taught. This is a great time saver, and if more than one person teaches the same class, the sets can be shared. When previously developed transparencies are being used, they must be reviewed for dated material. New transparencies should be made when necessary.

Another piece of AV equipment that is useful is the slide projector. Slides can be taken of almost anything, including catalog cards, pages of indexes, library service areas, and patrons actually using the materials within the library. Slides can be arranged in a sequence that supports the lecture being given. By manually controlling the slide projector, the instructor can show each slide when desired. Also, most slide projectors allow for backward and forward movement. This is especially helpful when there are questions that involve a previous slide. Some slide projectors can be synchronized to a tape player. This allows for a lecture or discussion to be put on tape and then synchronized to the slides. Slide-tape programs are particularly good for self-instruction or as a change of pace in the classroom. They can also be chosen for stationary orientation tours and point-of-use instruction.

Essential for both the overhead and the slide projector is a projection screen. Using the painted walls is usually not satisfactory because of the glare that bounces back. Permanently mounted wall screens are desirable for a classroom. A portable screen, however, will allow for greater flexibility, especially if one screen must be used in more than one area. There are many types of screens, and care should be taken to choose one that fits the lighting conditions of the rooms being used.

As its name implies, the opaque projector is able to project opaque material. This includes such items as the page of a book, a card from the card catalog, or pages from indexes. In addition to projecting material, the opaque projector can be

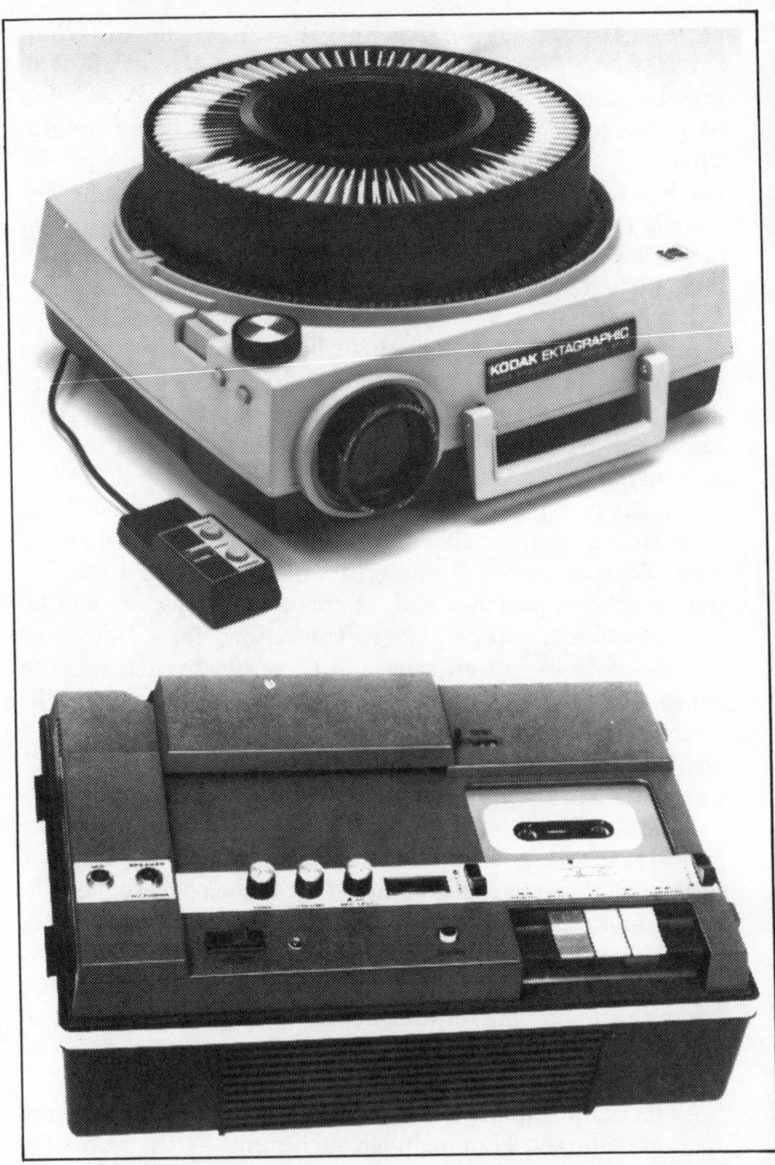

Slide projector courtesy of Eastman Kodak Company, Motion Picture and Audiovisual Markets Division. Cassette recorder/player courtesy of Telex.

used to enlarge drawings for posters or displays. These projectors are not as versatile as slide or overhead projectors and tend to be more cumbersome to use. Often the images are not clear, and it takes more effort to project the material properly. With some models, there is also the danger of scorching the material being projected, as a result of the intense heat being given off. Great care should be taken with valuable material such as manuscripts or rare books.

Movie and filmstrip projectors are probably the least used in a library program. Very few commercial products are suitable at the postsecondary level, and in-house products tend to be prohibitive in terms of both time and capital. Also, these media are difficult to update.

Videotape units are the most expensive investment of all the AV equipment listed. To view a videotape there must be a television monitor and a videoplayer. If videotapes are to be made, there must also be camera equipment for filming. Videotape does have the advantage of being able to record and film complete class lectures. This is beneficial if the same lecture can then be shown to multisectioned classes. Other instructional areas have often made use of videotapes for large group lectures in biology, western civilization, history, and so on. Another very good use for videotapes is for teacher evaluation. This technique has been used for many years in teaching practicums. Librarians are able to watch themselves in front of a class and evaluate their presentations. This is especially useful for those just beginning to teach.

Headsets or earphones can be used for self-instruction programs. If a slide-tape program is available, a student can plug a headset into the appropriate jack on the tape recorder and listen to the program without disturbing others. Headsets are necessary if AV material will be used in public areas of the library.

The final item mentioned in the list of possible equipment is a sound projector with a built-in screen. This is a portable unit that has the ability of showing slide-tape programs on a relatively small screen. There is a jack for a headset, thus

making it an ideal unit for self-instruction programs. This projector can also be used for stationary orientation tours, point-of-use programs, or for general slide-tape programs such as "Using the Library for Research" or "Business Reference Sources."

To summarize, AV equipment is quite appropriate for use in an academic library instructional program. It isn't necessary for an instructional program to have every piece of equipment listed above. One library may find that four overhead projectors will be more beneficial than one videotape player. Individual preferences may dictate what should be ordered or purchased. However, having the basic equipment available for use provides the potential for flexible and dynamic classes and programs.

THE QUESTION OF MECHANICAL ABILITY

Since librarians in general have had minimal experience with AV equipment, they are not comfortable with the idea of using it. Many claim that they aren't "mechanically inclined," and this keeps them from making use of media. It should be reassuring that it doesn't take any special ability to use AV, only practice with the machines. No one should attempt to use a piece of equipment in the classroom with which he or she does not feel comfortable. Practice turning the overhead on and off. Try various transparencies on the machine. Move the overhead or slide projector to different positions in the room. Sit at a few locations in the room and see if the slides or transparencies are clear and in focus. Practice lecturing with the equipment. Make sure that the slide projector and tape player are connected correctly. Check the sound levels. In other words, feel totally at ease with the equipment, or it will be just one more reason to worry about your presentation.

If there are a number of librarians who are unfamiliar

Facing Page: Slide projector "Caramate," courtesy of Singer Education Division. Overhead projector "Specialist," courtesy of Bell & Howell.

with the various pieces of equipment, the coordinator could arrange a workshop or seminar that will provide information on the use of the equipment and the opportunity for hands-on experience. If there isn't an "expert" in-house, it may be possible to have someone from the outside present the material and explain the machines.

THE MANAGEMENT OF AV MATERIALS AND EQUIPMENT

Although this discussion presumes a certain independence on the part of each librarian, there should be someone ultimately responsible for the equipment. If the equipment is ordered from the AV service on campus, the service is responsible for scheduling, delivery, pickup, and repairs. Some services also provide someone to operate the machines. If the library has its own equipment, these same activities must be done. An individual or office should be in charge of scheduling and repairs. Most libraries lack the personnel to deliver and/or operate the equipment. The most logical office or person would be that of the instructional coordinator.

No matter who is assigned responsibility, the first thing to be completed is an inventory of what AV equipment is available for use and where this equipment is stored. It is a revelation to see just how much a library does have on hand. At the same time the inventory is made, a list should be kept of models and model numbers of each item. A file of operating manuals should be established so that repair information can be readily found.

Once the inventory is complete, policy and procedure should be established and included in the policy manual for the overall instructional program. Information should include what equipment is available, how to reserve it, and what to do if the equipment fails to operate. The office or individual responsible should keep some type of checkout system. It is quite effective to have a desk calendar that has the hours of the day listed. Individuals can then reserve the piece of equipment needed for the day and time desired. Scheduling conflicts can then be avoided.

Everyone using the equipment should be reminded to report all mechanical problems *immediately*. Broken equipment should be repaired as quickly as possible and replacement items such as bulbs should be kept in stock. The equipment should be cleaned and inspected on a regular basis.

One more concern about equipment is storage. It is safest to have a secure area—preferably one with a lock—for keeping equipment. Having equipment kept in the instructional classroom can also work. However, if there are many different pieces, storing them in a classroom can limit access when classes are in session. Also, there may be vandalism if they are stored in the open.

In deciding about a storage area, careful thought should be given to temperature control. Equipment should not be stored in humid or damp places. Also, extreme heat or cold can seriously affect slides, films, and transparencies. Another consideration is transporting equipment. Slide and overhead projectors have bulbs that tend to loosen or need more frequent replacement if the machines are not carefully transported. Having appropriate AV carts can help to alleviate this problem.

Almost all of these activities regarding AV equipment can be handled by a clerical or student worker. A clerical worker is most often in the office for scheduling purposes. Equipment maintenance can be accomplished by a student working four or five hours per week. The instructional coordinator, although ultimately responsible, should be able to delegate the day-to-day details.

BUYING EQUIPMENT

There are many brands and types of equipment on the market. In fact, it can be a very confusing process to pick and choose dependable and durable equipment. The best advice that can be given is to talk with those on the campus whose departments already have equipment. Find out what is recommended, what problems they have had with the machines, if there is one machine that should be avoided at all costs, and so forth. AV services will have records of the repairs on the various models and brands, and the personnel are usually quite frank about the worth of the various items.

There are also some catalogs and directories that will be beneficial for those in the market for equipment. The National Audio-Visual Association publishes an annual guide entitled *Audio-Visual Equipment Directory.*[2] This will show pictures of the equipment as well as list prices. The *Consumers Index to Product Evaluation and Information Sources*[3] does a good job of covering the consumer field, including those journals and magazines that review AV equipment. Other good sources are *EPIE Reports*[4] and *Library Literature* under the subject "Audio-visual Materials—Equipment and supplies."

Since library budgets tend to be tighter and tighter each year, it may be necessary to purchase one piece of equipment at a time. The opportunity to buy in bulk through the campus' AV service should be investigated. This may provide the library with a price break. An updated list of equipment that needs to be purchased should be kept at hand for those unexpected lump sums of money that must be spent quickly.

DEVELOPING AV MATERIAL

As mentioned earlier, the commercial market for AV material that supports postsecondary library instruction is virtually nonexistent. Academic librarians often find that materials developed for the high-school level are unsuitable. This has made it necessary for librarians to develop their own materials. Creating slide-tape programs and transparency sets is commonplace among instructional librarians.

For many librarians, developing AV material is a new

venture. Few have had formal training, and often expert advice must be sought from outside sources. For those attempting to learn the various techniques for developing AV, the best advice that can be given is to become involved in an AV materials course being offered on campus. Often this is given through the College of Education. Just sitting in on the sessions for such a course will be beneficial. For anyone thinking about developing any type of medium, borrow or purchase a copy of *AV Instruction: Technology, Media, and Methods.*[6] This basic text will provide detailed information necessary to develop in-house AV materials. It is also an excellent resource book for additional sources of information and provides step-by-step instruction on the operation of most AV equipment.

For those looking for more library-oriented information on the development of media, there are suggested readings included at the end of the chapter. It is worthwhile to peruse these articles because many of their authors will indicate the pitfalls to be avoided. In addition to the recommended readings, there is always the opportunity to borrow samples of the various types of media from the local clearinghouses or Project LOEX. Seeing what has been developed can be helpful in suggesting new ideas.

QUALITY CONTROL

No matter what type of medium is being developed, accuracy and high technical quality are of the utmost importance. To be specific, text for the audio portion of any slide/tape program or filmstrip should be carefully examined and edited. Inaccurate material should be removed; ambiguous or misleading statements reworded. It is necessary to review the material periodically and remove or change any statements that may have become dated.

The use of high-quality audio tapes is one safeguard against sound distortion. Users should be able to clearly hear what has been recorded. There are times when it is the equipment and not the tapes that are at fault. Cleaning and inspection should be routinely scheduled for the audio equipment. Dust and dirt build-up can cause damage to the machines and the tapes. If new audio equipment is being considered for purchase, careful attention should be paid to the distortion levels when the sound is turned up.

High-quality slides and filmstrips are important. Blurry or poorly developed material should not be used. If the slides or films become scratched or damaged, they should be replaced. In addition to the technical quality, the material being shown should be accurate. Like the audio tape text, filmstrip and slide programs must be reviewed and updated regularly.

Of all the media that individuals use, transparencies tend to be of the poorest quality. They are often made in haste and there is little consideration given to their technical quality. The greatest criticism of many transparencies is the fact that they cannot be read at a distance. Material is frequently reproduced directly from books and indexes and then projected on the screen. Since the overhead projector has a limited capability to enlarge, such copied material cannot be clearly read beyond the first or second row of the classroom. Efforts must be made to enlarge material being copied for transparencies. There are a number of ways to accomplish this. First, there are some copy machines that have an enlargement capability. This is probably the easiest method to use. If this approach is not feasible, a typewriter with primary type face works very well. Elite or pica type faces are usually not effective. A third option is to use hand lettering. This could be done with felt-tip pens, wax pencils, or press-on letters. Whatever the method, transparencies should be developed which, when projected, are clear and readable from all parts of the room.

In general, there are three questions that should be asked about any medium being developed or used:

1. Is the material being presented accurately?
2. If it's audio in nature, can it be clearly heard and understood?

3. If it's visual in nature, is it clear and can it be read by everyone?

The answer to each of these questions should be an unqualified "yes." Any other answer is just not acceptable if the medium is going to be used in a library instruction program.

FOOTNOTES

1. For a complete discussion of the methods for creating transparencies see James W. Brown, Richard B. Lewis, and Fred F. Harcleroad, *AV Instruction: Technology, Media, and Methods* (5th ed.; New York: McGraw-Hill, 1977), pp. 128–146.
2. *The Audio-Visual Equipment Directory* (Fairfax, Va.: National Audio-Visual Association), Annual.
3. *Consumers Index to Product Evaluation and Information Sources* (Ann Arbor: Pierian), Quarterly.
4. *EPIE Reports* (New York: Educational Products Information Exchange Institute), Quarterly.
5. *Library Literature* (New York: Wilson), Monthly.
6. James W. Brown, Richard B. Lewis, and Fred F. Harcleroad, *AV Instruction: Technology, Media, and Methods* (5th ed.; New York: Mc-Graw-Hill, 1977).

SUGGESTED READINGS

General Works

Cochran, Lida M. and Johnson, John. "Resource List of Information about Media Production." *Audiovisual Instruction* 19 (June 1974): 89–101.

Earnshaw, Frank. "An Example of Cooperative Development of Library-Use Instruction Programs," in John Lubans, Jr., ed., *Educating the Library User*, pp. 392–400. New York: Bowker, 1974.

Hardesty, Larry L. *Use of Slide/Tape Presentations in Academic Libraries*. New York: Jeffrey Norton, 1978.

Hardesty, Larry L. "Use of Slide-Tape Presentations in Academic

Libraries: A State-of-the-Art Survey." *Journal of Academic Librarianship* 3 (July 1977): 137-140.

Heroux, Ronald G. "Motion Picture in Library-Use Instruction," in John Lubans, Jr., ed., *Educating the Library User,* pp. 318-329. New York: Bowker, 1974.

Kusnerz, Peggy Ann and Miller, Marie, comps. *Audio-Visual Techniques and Library Instruction.* ERIC Educational Document Reproduction Service, 1975. ED 118 106.

Palmer, Millicent C. "Creating Slide-Tape Library Instruction: The Librarian's Role." *Drexel Library Quarterly* 8 (July 1972): 251-267.

Schramm, Jeanne and Stewart, Frances. "The Use of the Slide Presentation in Library Orientation," in Barbara Mertins, comp., *Bibliographic Instruction,* pp. 20-30. West Virginia Library Association. Working Conference of the College and University Section. ERIC Educational Document Reproduction Service, 1977. ED 144 582.

Schwartz, Philip John, comp. *The New Media in the Academic Library Orientation 1950-1972: An Annotated Bibliography.* ERIC Educational Document Reproduction Service, 1973. ED 071 682.

Stevens, Charles H. and Gardner, Jeffrey J. "Point-of-Use Library Instruction," in John Lubans, Jr., ed., *Educating the Library User,* pp. 269-278. New York: Bowker, 1974.

Directories

The Audio-Visual Equipment Directory. Fairfax, Va.: National Audio-Visual Association, Inc. Annual.

Audio-Visual Market Place. New York: Bowker. Annual.

Brown, James W., ed. *Educational Media Yearbook.* New York: Bowker. Annual.

Journals

Audiovisual Instruction. Washington, D.C.: Association for Educational Communication and Technology. Monthly.

Media and Methods. Philadelphia, Penn.: North American Publishing Co. 9/yr.

APPENDIX

Additional Sources of Information

Although it is not within the scope of this handbook to provide a comprehensive list of readings on academic library instruction, there are sources of information that should be mentioned. Some of these are classic studies; others are more recent titles that will help to provide a framework for library instruction. The list of bibliographies and periodical indexes will, it is hoped, provide direction for those readers wishing to pursue the vast amount of literature available. Finally, information concerning newsletters, instructional organizations, clearinghouses, and directories is provided so that there can be a means of ongoing interaction between colleagues in the field.

GENERAL READINGS

Bonn, George S. "Training Laymen in the Use of the Library," in Ralph Shaw, ed., *State of the Library Art,* vol. 2, pt. 1. New Brunswick, N.J.: Rutgers University Pr., 1960.

Branscomb, Harvie. *Teaching with Books: A Study of College Libraries*. Chicago: Association of American Colleges and American Library Association, 1940. Reprint: Hamden, Conn.: Shoe String, 1974.

Breivik, Patricia Senn. *Open Admissions and the Academic Library*. Chicago: American Library Association, 1977.

"Integrating Library Instruction in the College Curriculum" *Drexel Library Quarterly* 7: 171-378 (July-October 1971).

Knapp, Patricia B. *The Monteith College Library Experiment.* New York: Scarecrow, 1966.

Library Orientation Series: Papers Presented at the Annual Conference on Library Orientation for Academic Libraries. Ann Arbor: Pierian.

1. *Library Orientation,* 1972.
2. *A Challenge for Academic Libraries,* 1973.
3. *Planning and Developing a Library Orientation Program,* 1975.
4. *Evaluating Library Use Instruction,* 1975.
5. *Academic Library Instruction: Objectives, Programs, and Faculty Involvement,* 1975.
6. *Faculty Involvement in Library Instruction,* 1976.
7. *Library Instruction in the Seventies: State of the Art,* 1977.
8. *Putting Instruction in Its Place: In the Library and in the Library School,* 1978.
9. *Improving Library Instruction: How To Teach and How To Evaluate,* 1979.

Lubans, John Jr., ed. *Educating the Library User.* New York: Bowker, 1974.

———. *Progress in Educating the Library User.* New York: Bowker, 1978.

Miller, Wayne Stuart. *Library Use Instruction in Selected American Colleges.* Urbana, Ill.: University of Illinois Graduate School of Library Science, Occasional Papers No. 134, August 1978.

Werking, Richard H. "The Library and the College: Some Programs of Library Instruction." ERIC Educational Document Reproduction Service, 1976. ED 127 917.

HANDBOOKS FOR TEACHING LIBRARIANS

Finn, David, Ashby, Margaret, and Drury, Susan. *A Teaching Manual for Tutor-Librarians.* London: Library Association, 1978.

Fjallbrant, Nancy and Stevenson, Malcolm B. *User Education in Libraries.* Hamden, Conn.: Linnet Books, 1978.

BIBLIOGRAPHIES

Delgado, Hannelore Rader. "Library Orientation and Instruction—1975: An Annotated Review of the Literature." *Reference Services Review* 4:91-93 (October-December 1976).

Krier, Maureen. "Bibliographic Instruction: A Checklist of the Literature, 1931-1975." *Reference Services Review* 4: 7-31 (January-March 1976).

Lockwood, Deborah L. *Library Instruction: A Bibliography.* Westport, Conn.: Greenwood, 1979.

Rader, Hannelore B. "Bibliography on Library Orientation—1974." *Reference Services Review* 3:29-31 (January-March 1975).

Rader, Hannelore B. "Library Orientation and Instruction—1973: An Annotated Review of the Literature." *Reference Services Review* 2:91-93 (January-March 1974).

Rader, Hannelore B. "Library Orientation and Instruction—1976: An Annotated Review of the Literature." *Reference Services Review* 5: 41-44 (January-March 1977).

Rader, Hannelore B. "Library Orientation and Instruction—1977: An Annotated Review of the Literature." *Reference Services Review* 6: 45-51 (January-March 1978).

Rader, Hannelore B. "Library Orientation and Instruction—1978: An Annotated Review of the Literature." *Reference Services Review* 7: 45-56 (January-March 1979).

PERIODICAL INDEXES

Library Literature. New York: Wilson, 1921/32-. Bimonthly, with annual cumulation.

Continually indexes journals covering the field of librarianship. Articles on academic library instruction may be found under the subject heading "Instruction in library use—College and university students."

U.S. Educational Resources Information Center (ERIC). *Resources in Education.* Washington, D.C.: U.S. Department of Health, Education and Welfare, National Institue of Education, 1966-.

Many appropriate subject headings, such as "Library Instruction," "Library Programs," and "Library Guides," are used. This is an excellent source for samples as well as directories and reports concerning library instruction.

LIBRARY INSTRUCTION CLEARINGHOUSES

National

Library Orientation-Instruction Exchange (LOEX): Center for Educational Resources, Eastern Michigan University, Ypsilanti, MI 48197.

Library Instruction Materials Bank (LIMB): Information Officer for User Education, Library, Loughborough University of Technology, Loughborough, Leicestershire LE11 3TU, Great Britain.

Data Bank for User Education Materials: Chief Librarian, Cauldfield Institute of Technology, Victoria, Australia, 3145.

State and Regional

There are a number of state and regional clearinghouses that have been established in recent years. Due to the changing nature of such information as location, address, and contact personnel, any listing is quickly outdated. The latest list may be requested from Project LOEX. Listings can also be found in Luban's *Progress in Educating the Library User*, pp. 219-220, and Lockwood's *Library Instruction: A Bibliography*, pp. 9-13.

NEWSLETTERS

National

Library Orientation-Instruction Exchange (LOEX). *LOEX News*, quarterly, 1974-. (Project LOEX, Center of Educational Resources, Eastern Michigan University, Ypsilanti, MI 48197.)

Infuse, bimonthly, 1977-. (Information Officer for User Education, Library, Loughborough University of Technology, Loughborough, Leicestershire LE11 3TU, Great Britain.)

American Library Association. *Library Instruction Round Table Newsletter*, 1978-. Available free to members of A.L.A., Library Instruction Round Table.

State and Regional

Newsletters come in many different formats. Some are commercially printed while others are in-house publications. Frequently they are published by a state or regional library organization. The main purpose of such publications is to serve as a forum for communication. Like the clearinghouses, it is difficult to establish an accurate list of state and regional newsletters. It is recommended that Project LOEX be contacted for the latest list available. There is also a list in Luban's *Progress in Educating the Library User,* pp. 221-222, and Lockwood's *Library Instruction: A Bibliography,* pp. 9-13.

PROFESSIONAL ORGANIZATIONS

American Library Association, 50 East Huron St., Chicago, IL 60611.

A. American Library Association, Library Instruction Round Table.
B. American Library Assocation, Instruction in the Use of Libraries Committee.
C. Association of College and Research Libraries, Bibliographic Instruction Section.
D. Association of College and Research Libraries, Education and Behavioral Science Section. Committee on Bibliographic Instruction for Educators.
E. Association of College and Research Libraries, Junior College Section. Instruction and Use Committee.

State and Regional Library Associations.

State and regional library associations have recognized the need for special interest groups concerned with library instruction. Many of these organizations have not only formed structured committees, but they have produced directories of the various instructional activities being carried on in the state or region. For information regarding membership in such associations, the appropriate state or regional headquarters should be contacted.

Glossary of Bibliographic Instruction Terms

BIBLIOGRAPHIC INSTRUCTION	encompasses all activities designed to teach the user about library resources and research techniques.
CLEARINGHOUSE	a centrally located office which collects, screens, and organizes instructional material that has been developed. Such material can often be borrowed, and many of the clearinghouses have some type of newsletter that is sent to members. Library-instruction clearinghouses have been organized on national, state, and regional levels.
COMPUTER-ASSISTED INSTRUCTION	involves the use of the computer and computer technology for teaching library skills. Individuals learn by interacting with preprogrammed lessons.
COURSE-INTEGRATED INSTRUCTION	the objectives of a nonlibrary course include library instruction as an essential part of the course. Its importance is often demonstrated by its inclusion in the course of study for the class.

COURSE-RELATED INSTRUCTION	usually involves a single lecture given by the librarian. The instruction centers on the specific needs of the students in a particular class.
CREDIT INSTRUCTION	formal courses on library resources, research methodology, and information retrieval. It is formally recognized as a course by the college or univeristy and is often offered for one, two, or three credits.
LIBRARY ORIENTATION	activities that introduce patrons to the facilities, services, and policies of the library. Guided and self-guided tours are common examples of orientation activities.
"PATHFINDERS"	see "topical guides"
POINT-OF-USE INSTRUCTION	a detailed explanation of how to use a specific research tool. Such information is either in print or nonprint format and is located near the tool being explained. Point-of-use material would include a slide-tape program on *Psychological Abstracts* or *ERIC* or a printed handout on the *American Statistics Index*.
TOPICAL GUIDES	printed material that arranges in search-strategy order the basic resources available for doing research on a particular subject. "Pathfinders," copyright by Addison-Wesley, is a commercially produced series of topical guides that came out in the mid-1970s.

INDEX

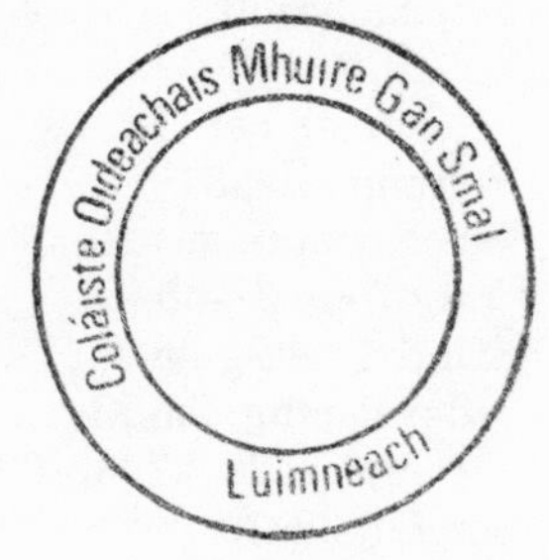

WITHDRAWN FROM STOCK